OCT – – 2007

NO RESERVATIONS

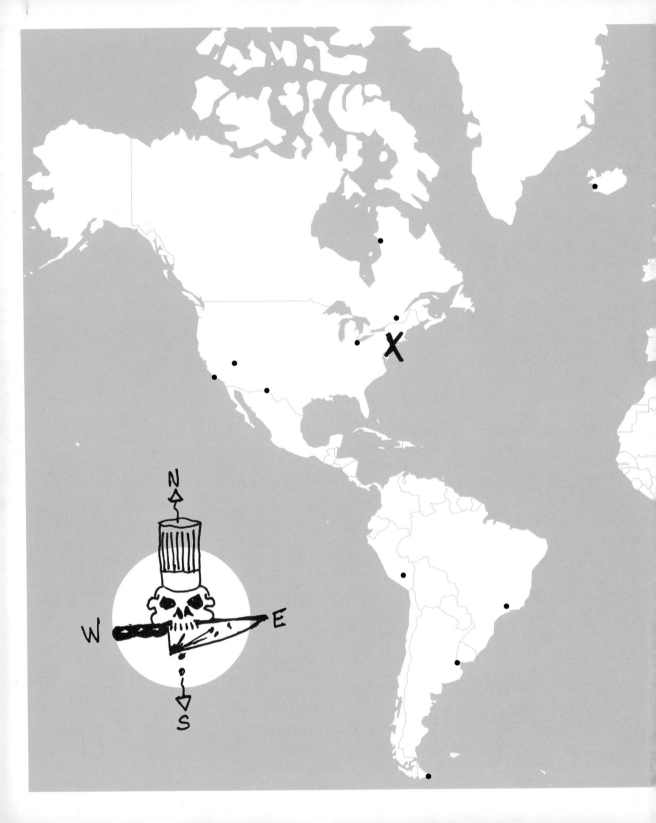

ANTHONY BOURDAIN
NO RESERVATIONS

AROUND THE WORLD
ON AN EMPTY STOMACH

BLOOMSBURY

Published by Bloomsbury USA, New York
Distributed to the trade by Holtzbrinck Publishers

All papers used by Bloomsbury USA are natural, recyclable products made from wood grown in well-managed forests. The manufacturing processes conform to the environmental regulations of the country of origin.

LIBRARY OF CONGRESS CATALOGING-IN-PUBLICATION DATA HAS BEEN APPLIED FOR.

ISBN-10 1-59691-447-5
ISBN-13 978-1-59691-447-6

Map on title page courtesy of University of Alabama
The Beirut chapter is reprinted with the permission of Salon.com, where it originally appeared in somewhat different form.

Photographs courtesy of The Travel Channel, L.L.C., and Tracey Gudwin

First U.S. Edition 2007

10 9 8 7 6 5 4 3 2 1

Designed and typeset by Elizabeth Van Itallie
Printed in the United States of America by Worzalla

TO ARIANE

CONTENTS

MEET THE BAND

When I became a cook, it felt like running away with the circus—or joining a rock-and-roll band (without having to know how to play guitar). As things turned out, I spent nearly the next three decades surrounded by malcontents, refugees, "borderline personalities," and misfits. And I liked it. No, *loved* it. But when I moved over into the presumably more civilized arena of television, I figured things were going to be different. For starters, I thought I'd be associating with—how can I say it?—a more *genteel*, well-adjusted class of people. No more late-night calls from bail bondsmen or frantic early-morning pleas for an "emergency" loan. In place of my usual foulmouthed crew of metalheads, *vatos locos*, and adrenalin junkies, there'd be nice, clean-living young grads from the NYU film school. We'd sit around like the cast of *Friends*, sipping half-caf mochaccinos and talking about Italian neorealist cinema.

Wrong! Instead, I got the *No Reservations* crew, a veritable control group for clinical study, a cabal of tightly wound, high-functioning screwheads, riddled with disturbing eccentricities, who have become—to my great pleasure and personal enrichment—my new dysfunctional family.

◄ **LYDIA TENAGLIA:** The Boss. The creative mastermind behind ZeroPointZero Production, Lydia produced, shot, and supervised the editing of most of the previous series, *A Cook's Tour*, where we all met—and defected with me to create *No Reservations*. Along with . . .

► **CHRIS COLLINS:** . . . her husband, and the third member of the evil troika from which this whole maniacal endeavor has sprung. Unlike Lydia, who has become a prisoner of success, forced to oversee the ever-expanding daily operations at ZPZ Central, Chris actually makes it out on the road with us every once in a while (if the bathrooms and the spaghetti Bolognese in the destination country look promising). It is useful to know that Chris's favorite director is Harold Ramis, that he believes *Meatballs* was a vastly underrated classic, and that there's nothing on earth that can't be improved by a good poop joke.

◄ **TRACEY GUDWIN:** Field producer and cameraperson. Tracey, whose outlook on life runs along the lines of "rainbows and unicorns," usually bears the full brunt of my crankiness, cynicism, and dissatisfaction—as well as my perverse impulses to emulate, say, the epic tracking shot from Orson Welles's *Touch of Evil*.

► **TODD LIEBLER:** Legendary cameraman, "B-roll king," and, increasingly, on-camera talent. Todd's obsessive need to constantly irrigate his system with vast amounts of bottled water leads to frequent interruptions in filming. And his less-than-graceful ways have led to tragedy, mishap, comedy—and an international reputation for destructive behavior.

◄ **DIANE SCHUTZ:** Assistant producer. Diane has dragged her relentlessly optimistic attitude and her bag of snacks across most of the globe by now. We have tried to break her good cheer for years—to no avail. If we were facing a firing squad, Diane would say, "At least their uniforms are nice!"

► **RENNIK SOHOLT:** Assistant producer. Rennik alternates with veteran Diane in researching, setting up, handling logistics, talent-wrangling, and keeping us all supplied with appropriate meds. Works like a demon, never sleeps, is frighteningly organized—and will probably climb a tower and start shooting strangers someday. Which makes him our kinda guy.

INTRODUCTION

Welcome to my life for the last three years: planes, trains, hotels, country inns, longboats, tents, jungle lodges, helicopters . . . and the many, many wonderful places in between. It's still a new life, completely unlike my old one, a dream, a little boy's fantasy of a job. It's what happened after everything changed for me.

In simplest terms, while bouncing around between twenty-eight countries, a continuing journey of nearly 200,000 miles, my crew took pictures. These are some of them. And every picture tells a story—not just my story, but the stories of the small crew who were there with me and of the people we encountered along the way. Of our subjects and the places they live and the way they live there—the things they love, the people they are—we get only tantalizing glimpses. We necessarily skim across the surface of the places we go, never staying long. We point our cameras, make a few observations, and move on. "I missed that," I'll say to myself afterward. "I didn't notice." Or I was too tired, sick, bored, frightened, or closely involved to see. Sometimes the truth about things reveals itself only when we look back at the photographs.

When we make *No Reservations*, we're very careful to not say, "Here's Ghana!"—or Portland, or Jaipur—"And here's what you need to know! This is what it's like!" We try instead to give viewers a brief taste, a sense of what we felt during the relatively short time we were there. We're not making shows about "The Best of India!" or "The Real India!"—and certainly not "The Comprehensive India," or anywhere else. India would be a life's work—and an unfinished one—no matter how long we spent there. But if we do our jobs right, after we've edited down all the snippets of tape and added a narration, those who watch the show get a suggestive glimpse of the places we go—can imagine what it feels like, sounds like, smells like to walk down a crowded street lined with food stalls in Jaipur or Hong Kong or Accra.

In these pictures, too, I hope you'll get the whiff of our travels. The smells of Southeast Asia, for instance: burning joss, jasmine flowers, the seductive reek of durian, pepper oil, fish sauce, and the exhaust from a million motorbikes. The call to evening prayer in rural Java: first the mullah's exhortation, then a response from somewhere in the distance, then another—and then suddenly the valley filling with voices, hundreds of farmers, still working their intricately terraced rice paddies, pausing to pray in place, the murmur coming from all directions in the darkening sky, ghostly and beautiful beyond words. The sounds of farmers waking in the predawn light in China, coughing and spitting before heading out to their fields; the lovely, hollow tones of bamboo wind chimes in Bali; the

constant *binggg . . . bonnngg . . . binggg* of instruments from unseen temples.

Here's the short version of how these pictures were taken, and by whom: *No Reservations* is the end product of a long process and the efforts of many people. I like to say that we're like a band, perpetually on the road, a small crew of five very close friends with tiny little cameras—no sound guy, no big microphones, no script girl, no script, no hair-and-makeup, and no trailer. And that's true enough. The road team has indeed come to resemble Spinal Tap on tour. The basic unit is me; Tracey Gudwin, who produces and also holds a camera; Todd Liebler, who shoots; another shooter, either Jerry Risius, or Zach Zamboni, or Mike Green, or Alan Weeks; and an assistant producer, either Diane Schutz, Rennik Soholt, or (recently) Tom Vitale. Every once in a while, Chris Collins, who heads up the production company with his wife, Lydia Tenaglia, will come out on the road and one of the above will sit it out. This is only right and good for my mental health—it was Chris and Lydia who got me into this whole TV thing in the first place. On a previous series, on another—less accepting, less good—network, the crew consisted of just me, Chris, and Lydia, and later, Diane. Chris and Lydia got married just a few days before setting out to shoot our first shows together in Japan, Vietnam, and Cambodia. They celebrated their honeymoon in Saigon, between scenes.

On location, we shoot anywhere from forty-five to seventy-five hours of tape between the three camera people. And generally, we know which of a number of brilliantly talented editors will be getting the footage when we return to New York. It is a particular joy, while shooting, say, along the Mexican border, to know that Eric Lasby is waiting to edit our stuff, that we can eventually tell him, "Make this episode look and sound like the early work of Robert Rodriguez! Like *El Mariachi*!" Or, when shooting in Yunnan Province in China, that Chris Martinez awaits, ready to cut, his work obsessively lyrical. We all know and love great films (and cheesy ones, for that matter) and ripping off our favorite directors for visual and audio cues—in search of a different and hopefully appropriate look and sound for each episode—is one of the most satisfying features of making the show. Shooting in Sicily? Let's steal that black-and-white Italian-ennui look from Antonioni's *L'Avventura*! Hong Kong? John Woo! Ringo Lam! New York? Let's rent an old Checker cab, shoot only at night, and do the early-Scorsese thing!

We want to make each episode as different from the one before as possible. To do this, of course, requires a combination of good luck, serious labor, and straight-up hustling. Television is, by nature, formulaic. If you make two or three shows and they do well, the people in airless offices whose money you've ruthlessly squandered to actually make those shows start to wonder, "Gee . . . what's working here? What is it exactly that people like about this thing? And how do we do it again?" It's an understandable impulse—to repeat what worked last time. In my old job, it was a mark of pride to knock out 150 pieces of onglet a night, each one perfect and each one exactly the same. But in this gig, that's something we fight very hard to avoid doing. That means there are "happy" shows and sad ones; sentimental, snarky, frightened ones; bitter, reflective, confused, surreal, impressionistic, philosophical, funny, and angry ones.

Even the content of the shows is up for grabs. Though I choose where we go and what we're ostensibly going to see and do, we never know what will actually happen when we get there. Some places are easy; I defy anyone with a working video camera and opposable thumbs to go into Indonesia and not come out with something good. But some efforts are total disasters, where everything—weather, logistics, sidekicks, and subjects—goes terribly wrong and events spin unpredictably out of control. Fortunately (or unfortunately) for me, this makes, I'm told, frequently entertaining television. Whether I'm rolling a thousand-pound ATV over myself in New Zealand, or jumping off a cliff into water of indeterminate depth in Sicily, or finding myself an awkward and unwilling dance partner to a eunuch with a five o' clock shadow, someone, somewhere, it appears, finds it amusing. I try very hard not to entertain in this way. A successful show, for me, is one where I meant every word—where, to quote Kurt Vonnegut, "everything was beautiful and nothing hurt."

But if a country sucked and I was downright miserable, I try to show that. If a city like Hong Kong feels to me like I'm living inside a psychedelic pinball machine, I want the episode to look that way. For me, Uzbekistan was a less fun and decidedly less emotional destination than, say, Malaysia. In Uzbekistan, we were surrounded by suspicious secret police, donkeys, giardia, bad food, and a culture of fear and paranoia. In Malaysia, I was coming off a very bittersweet personal experience, and the kindness and beauty of the Iban people in Borneo made me feel wistful and deeply moved. The resulting shows reflect those divergent attitudes.

Singapore and Iceland are two very different places, and I brought very different preconceptions and personal history to each of them. The show—to put it plainly—is proudly bipolar.

We are, all of us who make the show, fully aware that this ethic does not always result in satisfying television. But we have to assume that if you wanted the same thing night after night, you'd be watching the Barefoot Contessa instead of us.

When we make the show, whoever is assistant-producing carries a still camera and is tasked with taking production photographs for the Travel Channel website. Which means that Diane, or Rennik, or Tom has to remember—in addition to keeping track of shot camera tapes, wrangling local talent, getting us from place to place, making sure releases are signed, providing us with snacks and local beverages—to document the event. Depending on circumstances, and my moods, they do this with varying degrees of success. Thankfully, and rather remarkably, considering they're already hauling around a hefty video camera for ten or twelve hours a day, Todd and Tracey regularly manage to snap off an impressive number of shots on their personal cameras. That theirs are among the most beautiful shots in this book is unsurprising. They are, after all, professionals. They tend to pay attention to little things like focus, composition, and metering. But it's the "amateur" stuff that often tells the loudest stories. Diane's enthusiasm—and willingness to jam a camera into our faces in uncomfortable situations—has resulted in many "golden moments," however humiliated and homicidally enraged I might have felt at the time.

I'm of two minds about this book. On one hand, I know I'm happy to have it. It's a scrapbook of my life, for Chrissakes, so you'll forgive me for thinking it's the perfect thing to curl up with on the couch, relive all those times good and bad, remember all the friends I've made around the world—as well some of the goofballs and meatheads I'm glad never to be seeing again. Knowing that possibly thousands of people are going to see Chris Collins, as I did so many times, looking ridiculous—and having the opportunity to discuss some of his plumbing-related phobias—gives me a nice warm feeling of payback. On the other hand, I anticipate the inevitable reaction of some well-wishing fan of *Kitchen Confidential* who will approach me and say, "Dude! Didn't you used to write?! I mean, like . . . books . . . with words in them? You don't even cook anymore, dude! What's up?" Which is why I've done my very best to not make this some cynical, cheap-ass "companion" book to the series, filled—as those things so often are—with excerpts from voice-over scripts, a few maps, and a bunch of blurry photos taken from the show. You'll find in these pages a few helpful nuggets of hard-earned wisdom, useful tactics for travel and eating around the world. How to minimize the risk of gastrointestinal mishap, for instance—something at which all of us on the crew have become necessarily adept. I will point out from time to time specific places, features, and curiosities of the road, and tell you a bit about the best and worst places to visit and to eat—as I have found them. But principally, I'll show you what we saw as we moved back and forth and around this earth.

Looking at these photographs, I know that I will never understand the world I live in or fully know the places I've been. I've learned for sure only what I don't know—and how much I have to learn.

I have come to realize with certainty, however, that I have the best job in the world. And that I work with some of the finest people on it. To be able to go wherever I want, when I want, do what I want, and then tell stories about what I've experienced is an incredible privilege. Who gets to do what I do? And when you're that damned lucky, how do you stop? How do you ever get off the ride? And why would you? If one thing is clear to me about traveling perpetually, it's that it's a great gift. That as long as I'm allowed to do it, as long as Travel Channel is silly enough to pay for me to do it, as long as it's this much fun, I have to keep doing what I'm doing. If I have a single virtue, it's curiosity. It's a big world. Far bigger than I'd ever imagined—even as a boy reading adventure stories about pirates and castaways. I don't know where I'm going. Or when I'll stop.

But I know what I've seen.

I saw this . . .

ASIA

CHINA

Deep inside every great cook, no matter whether he's Italian, French, Brazilian, or American—anyone who knows what the good stuff is and what to do with it—lurks the heart and soul of a Chinese guy. There are no "good" and "bad" ingredients in China. There are the easy—usually expensive—ingredients. And then there's the real stuff—the stuff where it took maybe a few centuries of trial and error to figure out how to make it good or to discover what was good about it all along. Great French chefs know, for instance, that the fish's head is the best part. But they would seldom dare to serve it. In French restaurants in the U.S., they literally can't give it away. In China, cooks take it for granted that you will prefer the head. Who wouldn't? Chinese cooks and chefs are used to preparing food for customers who know what the fuck they're eating: what's good, where it's good, and when it's good. Next to them, we know nothing about food. We wallow in ignorance. Cave dwellers. Savages. Lucky for an occasional glimpse of light.

China alone would be a life's work, just noticing—not even, necessarily, understanding—the differences between regions, ethnicities, cuisines, and traditions. The episodes we filmed here and in Hong Kong represent the first delirious, glancing contact, a besotted, half-blind stumble up to the doors of a huge and ancient culture.

Rural Sichuan Province. Probably has fantastic cell phone reception—and wireless access.

It is no secret that I am besotted by Asia; that it's ruined me for the rest of the world; that all my over-romantic fantasies, all my movie-fueled expectations for the way a life well lived should be, converged and became real on repeated trips to Vietnam, Singapore, Malaysia, China, and Japan; that I later fell in love with Indonesia, Hong Kong—even not-so-pretty Taiwan and Korea. It's apparent in the shows. All of us who work on *No Reservations* have, to one extent or another, "gone bamboo." Scenes like this one, from a typical night out in Beijing, may help explain why.

(Above left) Noodle chefs. (Above right) Sichuan Province: An essential flavor. (Below) Outside of Chengdu: Craft services. The crew meal.

In the menu sign:

蚕　蛹 silk-worm 串 5
小鸡崽　香干 Xiao ji zai/xiang gan 串 5

(Above) Beijing street food. (Below left) Ever the professional, Chris is relentlessly thorough in his investigation of local culture. (Below right) Beijing: Todd relishes the prospect of slipping another needle into my foot while I'm immobilized during electro-acupuncture.

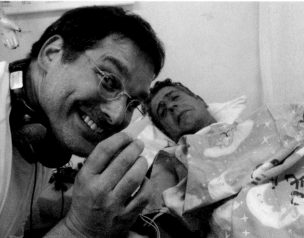

Sichuan Province.

The Himalayas: Yunnan Province, near Tibet. Altitude sickness. After two days and a night with my head pounding, I got smart and started sucking down canned oxygen. It helps. Dennis Hopper/*Blue Velvet* jokes ensued as I quickly became inseparable from my cans.

Hong Kong: "Wire Fu." I learn to "Keanu" with a team of stunt coordinators. The thirty-second fight sequence took about five hours to film.

Hong Kong: The noodle maker climbs on board his bamboo pole. This was probably the most breathtakingly beautiful food preparation scene I've ever seen. A lone old man, making noodles old style under the faded photographs of his parents, in a tiny, flour-dusted, rented apartment. So much work for so little . . . A method of noodle making that has nearly disappeared, even in China.

Kolkata: Believers cleanse
themselves in the Ganges. An
act of faith and devotion.

INDIA

There are two types of visitors to India: There are those who quickly find themselves frustrated, irritated, frightened of the food and water, intimidated by the great masses of humanity, overwhelmed by the all-too-evident poverty, ground down by the heat and the crowds, perplexed by the behavior of Indians. "What do they mean by that head waggle? I asked a direct yes-or-no question, dammit! What does that side-to-side toggling motion mean? And what the hell are you smiling at?"

Others, like me, are charmed. The famous smile and head waggle means, I have gathered, "I'm figuring out whether you are friend or foe—if you are a good person. I am considering an answer. I come in peace." You have to redefine words like "beautiful," "magnificent," and "gorgeous" when you travel through India. The forts and palaces and temples of Rajasthan, for instance, are so outsized in their opulence and grace as to short out the descriptive powers of the human brain. Even photographs don't do them justice.

I love India. I just don't know whether I can handle India. Whether I can wrap my tiny brain around its past, its present, or its future. Stand still with three video cameras in Kolkata or Mumbai and first two, then three, then twenty, then fifty people gather around to stare good-naturedly. You soon have a traffic problem

Kolkata: The flower market.

as people spill into the street. "What is your good name, sir?" people ask, perplexingly. Yet in the crowds—if you bother to look, really look—you see the future of the world. The two young men serving as your waiters at a *thali* meal in a dusty back street in Jaipur also study full time at university. They are completing their master's degrees in engineering. Their friends in America find MIT ridiculously easy. The rice farmer in the Sunderbans has a son in college too. To accept less than top marks would be the shame of the village. The heat and dust and smells of India either capture your heart—or repel you. But the colors—the saris, the spices, the fields and sky, rivers and lakes, the mountains and deserts—they stay with you forever.

Rajasthan: Mise en place.

(Above) Stoned outside the Bhang shop. (Below right) Spicy rice and sweet potatoes from a street vendor in Kolkata.

(Left) Mumbai: A moment of low comedy. Supposed to meet our local fixer and his friends for his birthday party at a swanky restaurant, we were "kidnapped" by our non-English-speaking driver, who, instead of taking us to our hotel to change clothes after a long, dusty shoot, drove us straight to the party. Mortified and embarrassed, Tracey and Diane tried valiantly to cover their shame by fashioning "skirts" from tablecloths. The effect, needless to say, was unimpressive. In the end, we did what we do best—said "Fuck it!" and behaved like idiots.

(Above) Kolkata: Down by the *ghats*, a group of men brush their teeth. (Below left) Udaipur: With His Excellency, the Maharana of Udaipur, at his palace. (Below right) "The Girls of *No Reservations*!" The mirrored chamber in my tower suite at the Devi Garh Hotel, near Udaipur.

(Opposite) **The Sunderbans: A rice-growing community in tiger country.** (Above) **An everyday scene in India.**

On the street in Jaisalmer. To the extent of our abilities, this is what the show is all about: a head-first full immersion in someplace that isn't very much like home. No Starbucks, no cash machines, no stage-managed "real-life encounters"—just an honest and direct recording of the way life is lived in the rest of the world. Moments like this make the show worth doing and, I hope, worth watching.

(Above left and right) Jaisalmer: The desert festival. (Below) The road to Jaisalmer: Another happy moment—when I am unreservedly delighted with my job, living in the moment, having a good time, nearly oblivious to the production van trailing me. This was one of those spur-of-the-moment, impulsive scenes. I saw a bus, its roof loaded with passengers and decided to join them. Up top was something of a party. There was singing, an offer of fruit, shared cigarettes. As we climbed down, an old man with a turban and an impressive Rajasthani mustache handed Jerry a handmade wallet and said, "Friend!" Though very poor, he refused to take money for it.

(Above) Outside Jaisalmer: I remember this moment. I was listening to a sad song on my iPod, and looking out at the desert while the crew shot B-roll footage of camels and landscape. I lay down and closed my eyes for few seconds, thinking about how strange my life had become, how far away I was from my old life, how distant from my old friends, how difficult it had become to connect with anyone who didn't do what I did, hadn't seen what I was seeing. When I opened my eyes and sat up, the song "Pets" by Porno for Pyros was still playing. Tracey was standing to my left, shooting me. A few yards to the right, Todd kneeled, also with a camera pointed in my direction. I swept my eyes slowly to the right and there was Jerry, sitting atop a camel—also shooting me. I laughed at the bittersweet freakshow my life had become. And then thought, These are my friends now.

INDONESIA

I've discovered a common thread between some places I really like: I love rice-growing communities—and rice farmers. Whether in Vietnam, the Sunderbans of West Bengal, or Java, Indonesia, there's something that hooks me about the cultivation of rice. It's beautiful, of course, the rice paddy. And becomes even more so on further inspection, when you realize the various dike-and-dam systems necessary to move water where it's needed, to keep it in or out; the many sections, each with different colors, for the stages of the growing process. Rice farmers work harder than just about anyone in the world, bent at the hip all day in ankle-deep water or mud, yanking or planting tiny handfuls of shoots, or replanting them. They hardly have time to concern themselves with aesthetics or landscaping. Yet, there are few things more breathtakingly, punch-in-the-chest lovely than a vista of Javanese rice terraces, the way the long, sinewy paddies, bright bright green, curve and swoop in emanating concentric rings around the natural features of the landscape. This is it, you think. It doesn't get any prettier than this.

Rice-farming culture, though—the basic nature of rice farmers—is, I have found, even more beautiful. The hard logistics of irrigation—multiple farmers relying on one water source, the need to share labor during the harvest, the fundamental need

Bali: Kememuk Falls, outside of Ubud.

to cooperate with others—seem to have made rice farmers, of all the world's callings, the most hospitable, no-bullshit, humble, and fun people on earth. The fiercest of guerrilla fighters during times of war, they are the most warm and welcoming in peace.

(Above) Java: Durian fruit, the notoriously foul-smelling, much-loved stinkfruit of Southeast Asia. They tie these weighty, armor-covered beasts to the trees, as they can kill you if they fall on you. Their gassy, semi-putrid odor can be smelled blocks away. Illegal to take on most forms of public transportation, forbidden in hotel rooms, thay have a flavor that has been described as "like eating custard in a lavatory." I like 'em! (Right) Java: One of those rare moments I live for. Perfection. A terraced rice paddy near Garut. Life looks, smells, and sounds like the movies. Like my dreams. There's nothing to say. Even the camera people shut up. We just look, and roll tape, in wonder . . .

Java: The Strongest Ram Contest. The sound of these enthusiastically competitive beasts colliding is unbelievable.

44

Bali: One of many, many festivals and ceremonies one is likely to encounter in Balinese daily life.

Java: A sad inevitability of my career is that wherever I go, I am, as honored guest with cameras pointing at him, asked to dance in public. Few things are more terrifying to me—and few things uglier and more pathetic to watch. Here, in an all-too-typical moment, I was sitting happily among the swelling crowd of townspeople, watching a contest of strength between rams, when the music started and the tiny, graceful dancer approached. Despite my fervent protestations, she dragged me into the center of the ring and tugged my gigantic, hideously awkward frame in front of the whole village. I felt like Peter Boyle in *Young Frankenstein*. I think that in this shot, I'm trying to distract the dancer by pointing at something in the distance— so I can run away. My ears still turn red looking at this.

Garut: The "Pancake Man" rows over to my hut.

(Above) Ubud: In a world of delicious roast pigs—and I've sampled a lot of them—this is the best I've ever had. Stuffed with herbs, slowly spit-roasted over low wood flame while constantly basted with coconut water—it is far and away the most glorious example of the pork-related arts. (Below) Bali: The "monkey dance."

INDONESIA: HOME OF SOME OF THE MOST HOSPITABLE, NO-BULLSHIT, HUMBLE, AND FUN PEOPLE ON EARTH.

(Above) Java: Todd, not the most nimble of men even at his best, has just knocked down the entire day's supply of food at an Indonesian Padang, a restaurant where the offerings are painstakingly stacked in an elaborate window display. Trying to get a close-up "beauty shot" of the food, he rammed his boom microphone into a supporting plate and the whole pyramid came crashing down, showering even the open backup containers with broken crockery. Not seen in this photo is the crowd of notables and elders from the local Islamic Society, who were waiting patiently at a table for their food. Naturally, we paid the damage for this awkward incident—and made a scene out of it in the show. Todd has never lived it down. We'll never let him. (Below) Todd tries to make amends by cleaning up. A year later, traveling around China, he was recognized by a number of Chinese and Singaporean fans, all pointing and exclaiming, "You!! You Mr. Clumsy Man!!"

Java: The carefully balanced beauty of a rice-growing community. In a country with seven thousand kinds of rice—and at least six names for its various forms—cultivation is almost indistinguishable from life itself.

JAPAN

I have a half-assed theory about Japan: that there's a direct relationship between the fetishism of the Japanese male—the kooky, fanatical, even sinister mix of unbridled enthusiasm and apparent reticence—and the spirit of exacting artisanship that makes Japan's cuisine so damn good, its architecture and design and customs so refined. It's as if Japanese men, all too aware that deep inside they'd like to stomp Tokyo flat, breathe fire, and do truly terrible and disgusting things to women, have built themselves the most beautiful of prisons for their rampaging ids. Instead of indulging their fantasies, they focus on food, or landscaping, or the perfect cup of tea—or a single slab of raw o-toro tuna—letting themselves go only at baseball games and office parties.

That's one theory anyway. Our Osaka show, where we investigated—and indulged in—the peculiar tradition of *kuidaore* (the pursuit of happiness through overindulgence—literally, bankrupting oneself through food and drink) was a delightfully illuminating example. Once forbidden, as lowly members of the merchant class, to exhibit conspicuous displays of material wealth, Osakans channeled their acquisitive impulses into the proud consumption of tasty things to eat. And drink.

Kiso Valley: A "cleansing ceremony" under a freezing waterfall. Idea is, you stand or sit there, with melting glacier drumming down on you—for as long as you can take it.

(Above left) Kiso Valley: Tracey's birthday party at an *izakaya*. We later heard she threw up on herself in the *onsen* (communal bath). This probably did not make a favorable impression on the fastidious Japanese. (Above center) Michiko Zento, our fixer (and old friend). (Above right) Michiko and I sit outside our hosts' house during Obon festival, summoning the ancestors, helping to guide them home. (Below) Osaka: Where to eat next?

(Above) My kooky *manzai* (slapstick comedian) friends and I eat our way across Osaka. (Below) Chris was expecting a gentle slap from a paper fan our hosts had given us. The bottle came as a surprise.

OSAKA, WHERE NEAR-LETHAL QUANTITIES OF FOOD AND DRINK ARE THE LOCAL CUSTOM.

Nari expresses her
love for kimchi.

KOREA

Has anyone ever been happier to be on the road with *No Reservations* than our office manager, Nari Kye? I don't think so. After months and months of being hectored every time I stepped into the damned office—"When are you going to go to Korea? When are you going to Korea?"—I finally decided to build an episode around our hyperactive, hyperenthusiastic, Korean American staff member. She proceeded to run the veteran eaters and travelers into the ground, outeating, outdrinking, and outpartying all of us, never losing her energy or her good cheer. Just when we were getting tired, she made it all fun again.

Seoul at night.

(Above) Tae Kwan Do school. Repeated takes of this face kick did me no good. (Below left) An imperial-style meal with Nari that never made it into the show. (Below right) Jerry sings "Anarchy in the U.K." at the crew's karaoke wrap party. His version of "(Can You Take Me to) Funkytown" is a classic.

(Above and below) A happy moment. Jerry, Nari, Tracey, and I eat barbecued pork—one of the rare instances when I continued to eat after the shoot was done. It was delicious.

IN NARI'S SLIPSTREAM, KOREA WAS A NONSTOP MARATHON OF FOOD, FAMILY, AND ROUND-THE-CLOCK RICE WHISKEY.

(Opposite) **Kimchi fermenting in clay pots. The heart and soul of Korean cooking.** (This page) **Nari in traditional dress, getting ready to pay respect to her grandfather.**

MALAYSIA

I've got some history in Malaysia—none of which I'll go into here. But suffice to say, I was in a very emotional, very shook-up place in my life when I arrived there again. I was, I realize now—and dimly understood even then—at some kind of crossroads in my life. I was going to either come out of it alive and maybe a little bit smarter—or sink back into ever darker territory.

When I see that episode now, the final scenes in particular, as I waited to be flown out of the jungle, I recognize a deep ambivalence about the future—about everything I had thought previously or believed to be true. I felt humbled, grateful, confused, and deeply wounded, all at the same time. The tattoo I had done in Kuala Lumpur, earlier in the show, I know now to have been an act of self-immolation. I felt as bad as I'd ever felt, and I wanted to remember it, commemorate it—to punish myself, so that hopefully I wouldn't make the same mistake again.

The Malaysia episode was titled "Into the Jungle"—and so it was, our first real trip into deep, deep bush. We traveled by boat up the river into Sarawak, on Borneo, chased former headhunters through overgrowth, up slippery inclines, down into vine-choked ravines, up and down and up and down—for miles. We waded over treacherous polished stones through jungle rivers, yanked leeches from our nether regions, drank deep of the local beverages.

Borneo: The river.

And I killed a pig. There was no graceful way out.

When the chiefs hand you a spear and suggest that as honored guest, you must pay tribute to both dinner and your hosts, you do it. You have to. It was one of the most difficult things I've ever done. Tracey, shooting the execution by the river's edge, was fine until she looked down and saw she was ankle-deep in blood. Me? I wanted to cry. I realized I'd lost something. Learned something terrible about the real cost of dinner.

I see something very different, I'm sure, than most viewers when I watch the Malaysia show. I'm pretty confident it's one of the best episodes we've ever done. But there's so much between the lines, invisible in plain sight—and of no interest to anybody but me—that I don't really have any perspective on it at all. I think it's good. I think it's beautiful.

I'll go back and visit my Iban friends one of these days. I promised the chiefs that I'd attend a harvest festival. Maybe get a happier tattoo this time.

A tough shoot. Chris and Todd (and Tracey, behind them) try to keep up with our Iban hosts as we trek through the jungle—at this moment, using the river because the foliage was so thick. The river bottom was covered with large, extremely slippery stones and the going was very, very difficult, not least because of the leeches, one of which attached itself to Tracey's ass. And of course we documented the event.

(Above) Sarawak, Borneo: David, our Malaysian fixer, and I pause for a meal during our trek. (Below left) An Iban prepares the pig I've just stabbed through the heart with a spear. (Below right) Diane bathes in the river.

(Above) Sarawak, Borneo: In the jungle, our host, an Iban chief, a former scout and human tracker for the Brits and a onetime head-hunter, pauses to grab us a snack of heart of palm.

(Left) I didn't teach this hand gesture to these kids. This particular tribe is seldom visited by outsiders. The few who do manage to make it this far upriver are tattoo enthusiasts and artists from America and Germany. The Iban are happy to show them their traditional hand-tap tattooing method and the proud history of their lives and travels and accomplishments on their bodies. In return, the visitors often tattoo their hosts. You'll see a chief covered with flowers and fish and the symbols of his people—with an incongruous screaming eagle or a skull with a top hat in between: a gift from a guest. The visitors left this charming middle-finger greeting behind as well.

(Above left) The entrance to the Batu caves. (Above right) Inside the caves, just after a blessing at the Hindu shrine. (Below) Sarawak, Borneo: Enjoying a drink with the chiefs of the Iban. A very happy moment in the longhouse. The man with his back to me has taken three heads, I was told, evidenced by the rings tattooed on his fingers (one for each head). You could scarcely find lovelier, gentler, or more hospitable hosts. Elsewhere, farther down the communal longhouse, families lay together on woven mats—Mom, Dad, and children just cuddling, passing the time. (Opposite) An Iban woman dances.

Once the launching point for the fearsome Sarawak Rangers, a native defense force organized by the British, the river is now the superhighway of Sarawak.

TAHITI

What little boy hasn't dreamed of the South Seas? Of the approach to a mysterious island, tattooed natives, crumbling tiki heads in the jungle, the mist-draped peaks of mountains that drop suddenly into dark, verdant valleys or churning sea? Who hasn't seen that movie about Gauguin, or seen his paintings from Hiva Oa, and thought, I'd like to do that! Just throw it all away and run off to Tahiti, paint, go barefoot, and copulate for the rest of my years.

Well, it wasn't exactly like that. (As I found out, it wasn't like that even in Gauguin's time.) Papeete, on Tahiti's main island, was much like any other French vacation community—with all the good and bad that implies. But Hiva Oa and the remote "motus" of Rangiroa were everything I'd dreamed of. The end of the world, Polynesian style. A remote, South Seas paradise, on a narrow spit of coral on the far side of an atoll, accessible only by boat. No power, no TV, no luxuries. But nice bathrooms! Just a thatch-roofed hut on a lovely beach and no distractions. Nothing to do but swim, fish, lay around in a hammock, and dream . . .

(Above) The Marquesas: Looking down into the steep interior valleys of Hiva Oa. (Opposite) A blissed-out moment on an otherwise surprisingly difficult shoot,

Rangiroa: A coconut crab in captivity. The hard-to-find crabs crack open coconuts with their powerful claws and eat the meat inside. Their own flesh and fat takes on a sweet flavor, much prized by locals. (Opposite) Hiva Oa, the Marquesas: *Copia* (coconut) drying in the sun. Copia is the one of the islands' only remaining exports—and one of a very few sources of income for the Marquesans outside of tourism. The French support the price as a form of stealth welfare.

Rae-raes, young men who, in keeping with Tahitian tradition, have been raised as women, feed me *poisson cru* (raw tuna tossed with coconut milk) at a local food stall.

THE MARQUESAS: NOTHING TO DO BUT SWIM, FISH, LAY AROUND IN A HAMMOCK, AND DREAM . . .

Our guide arrives with lunch.

(Above left) New shooter Zach collapses after a four-hour run through the jungle on horseback, shooting backward with his camera. (Above right) A tiki head, this one depicting a woman giving birth in the surf. (Below) Hiva Oa, the Marquesas: A new addition to my collection of tattoos—this one a traditional tiki design. Hey! It's the birthplace of the tattoo as we know it, where Western sailors first encountered the art form. How could I resist? (Opposite) Gauguin's grave.

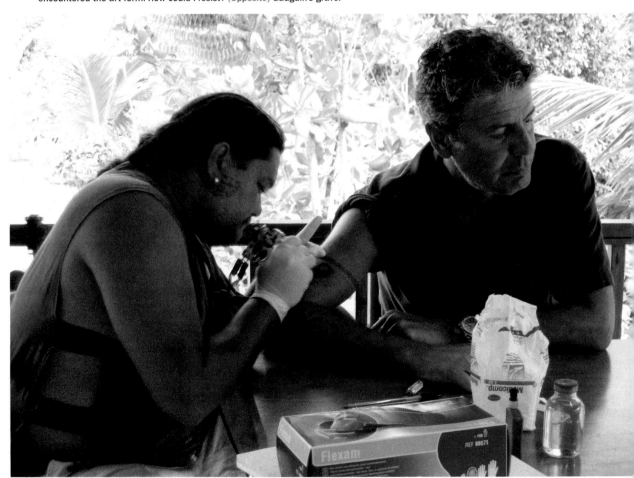

The absolutely delicious steamed shark's head at Macpherson Center.

SINGAPORE

If you've always wanted to go to Asia, but find yourself intimidated by the difference in culture, manners, and customs, maybe Singapore, or Asia Lite, is a sensible first foray—a veritable primer for later forays into India, Malaysia, or China. It's famously safe, clean, small, and English-speaking. Getting around is ridiculously easy. And you can gobble up the best of Chinese, Indian, and Malay specialties all in one place—easily, accessibly, and cheaply. It's one of the most food-centric, food-obsessed, food-crazy cultures on earth. At any gathering with locals, someone will suggest what you should be eating, where you should get it, and how to eat it when you're there. And while enjoying, say, chili crab at one place, you are likely to find yourself in a good-natured argument about the next place you should go—to eat *ba ku teh*, or chicken rice, or fettucine carbonara. Singapore's vibrant culture of hawker stands, eating houses, food courts, and *kopitiams* (coffee shops) makes it, along with Hong Kong, one of the world's two premier food destinations.

(Opposite) An eater's paradise. Macpherson Center is a typical Singaporean food court of "eating houses," hawker stands, and *kopitiams* (coffee shops)—basically a big communal area lined with small business with open kitchens, each with a different specialty. The Chinese chef here, in numerous trips to the fish market, asked the simple question: "You sell shark fin. You sell shark meat. Where is the head?" And thus was born the sublime, sticky, cartilaginous sweetness of his signature steamed shark head with soy and spring onions. What was once worthless is now an expensive treat. (Above) Crab bee hoon at Sin Huat Eating House in Geylang.

Sri Mariamman Temple, in Singapore's Chinatown.

Todd warns me of the dangers of smoking. Nothing like a photo of cancerous gums on your cigarette pack to make that butt taste even more delicious.

UZBEKISTAN

Tashkent. The phone rings in my hotel room. It's two in the morning, and I've just checked in and promptly collapsed into bed, exhausted after a long flight. The voice on the other end is the concierge, speaking with a thick accent. "You want massage? You want girl?"

No, I explain, I would not like a massage—or a girl. I am sleeping, and would like very much to continue sleeping.

Forty-five minutes later, there's a knock on the door. A thick-necked bruiser with blonde hair, dead eyes, and pink lipstick is standing in the hall.

"You want massage?"

How do you say "hepatitis C" in Uzbek? I can't remember. I slam the door, stumble back to bed, and jam the pillow over my face.

Welcome to Uzbekistan.

"Can we take your photo? Photo?"

In Uzbekistan, that request is almost universally met with a vigorously waved hand, a brief look of annoyance—and fear. Particularly after they get a load of the posse of current and former secret policemen posing as our "drivers" and "guides." This becomes apparent at one of the ubiquitous security checkpoints, where the various employees of various security organs gather to play Whose Dick Is Bigger. A beefy security guy rousts us from the vehicle. Our guys offer a quiet word or two. They argue. Finally, the athletic-looking driver of our

(Above) Samarqand. (Below left) Tashkent: Friday prayers at the mosque. (Opposite left) Plov. This example of Uzbek food is about as good as it gets. Which ain't that good, to be honest. (Opposite right) *Samsa* (dumpling) vendor.

IN UZBEKISTAN, YOU CAN GET ANYTHING YOU WANT TO EAT— AS LONG AS WHAT YOU WANT IS KEBAB OR PLOV.

production van steps up, smiling. Everybody knows him. Somebody served with him in the Soviet Spetsnaz. Back slaps. Smiles. Waves. We're through . . .

The statues of Stalin have been pulled down and replaced with statues of Tamerlane. But otherwise it's pretty much business as usual. The Maximum Leader's portrait is on the wall of every home and business. And unlike most autocrats in state portraiture, he doesn't even try to look like a nice guy. He looks like he's annoyed. Like he's been interrupted while observing a torture session—and he's unhappy about it.

As for the food: Care for some kebab? Plov? How about more kebab? Or some kebab?

Am I being dismissive of one of the original cradles of civilization? A onetime island of enlightenment, learning, art, and religion? A vital stop on the Silk Road, still beautiful with its mosques and arcades, its majestic, unforgiving steppes? The Soviets nearly ruined this place. Their ugly, soul-withering municipal buildings, the scars left by their propensity to lop off minarets, their management structure—even some of the same per-

sonnel—remain. It's an Islamic country where Islam is seen as a threat by the government. So everybody and everything is suspect. The appearance of a camera is never a good thing in Uzbekistan. Getting someone to sign a release—or any piece of paper, for that matter—is near impossible. It's probably a trick. Later, in a dark cell, I'll be confronted with that signature—attached to a confession. One of our secret police guides shows up one day with two black eyes. He says he walked into a door.

And yet, and yet . . . you look at the graceful sweep of the ancient architecture, take in the intricacies of the tile work, the endlessly repeated design features, and can't help but be enthralled by the devotion it must have required to make these things. At Friday prayers at a neighborhood mosque, there's a gentler Islam than the one you see on television. The children, of course, are the same as everywhere. Old men drink tea and smoke in the fading afternoon light. The young bride and groom at an Uzbek wedding, the same nervous expressions as newlyweds anywhere. We are so different. We are the same.

(Above) Me and my old buddy Zamir, the ultimate fixer and a good friend. Is there anything Zamir can't do? From St. Petersburg to Samarqand, he walks through walls and across borders. Wanna meet the KGB officer who recruited Aldrich Ames and Robert Hanssen? Zamir's your guy. Attend a traditional Uzbek wedding? He knows somebody. Dinner with Miss Russia? Zamir. Meet the Mafiya? Guess who can help? On the other hand, he tricked me into the excruciating "Uzbek massage," for which I'll never forgive him. (Opposite) *Midnight Express II* at a traditional hamam (an Arab-style sauna). The single most painful, embarrassing, and shameful episode of my life. This was not a massage. This was torture. The freak you see rear-mounting me twisted, yanked, bent, snapped, and pounded every muscle, bone, and tendon in my body. Fortunately, I was so busy trying not to scream that I was unaware of the sexual-humiliation component. I'm told the resulting footage was very funny. Believe me, I didn't think so at the time.

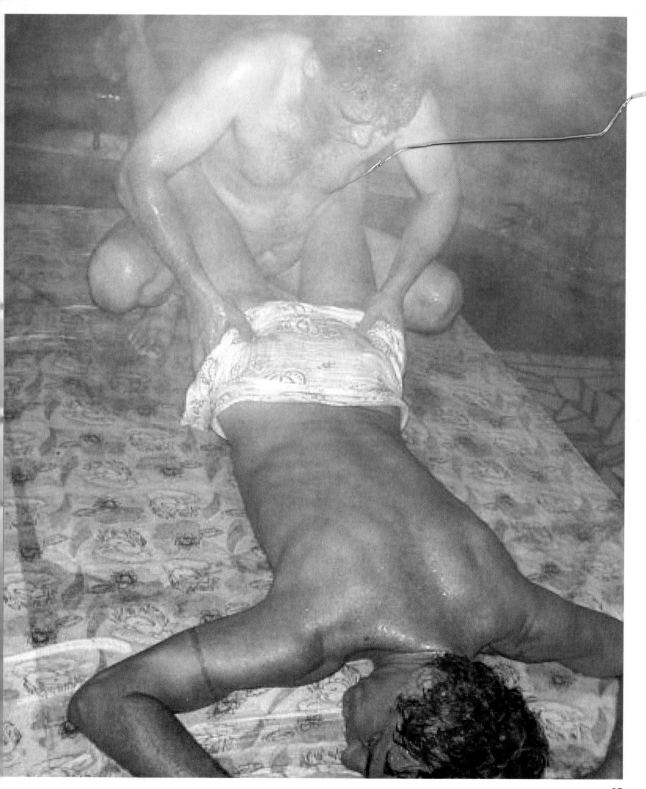

AFRI

CA

GHANA

Accra: The 31st December Makola Market.

At the airport in Accra, five spanking-new, jet-black SUVs with tinted windows were waiting on the tarmac to whip us past customs and immigration. In convoy, horns honking, we charged down the center of the road, traffic lurching onto the shoulders to get out of our way. We were accompanied at all times by a platoon of drivers, escorts, and sunglassed officials from the ministry of tourism, our whole trip organized and choreographed with military precision. An army helicopter ferried us over thick jungle and thatch-roofed villages; schoolchildren poured from one-room schoolhouses to watch our approach.

Ordinarily, it's everything we hate and try to avoid: working with government agencies and tourist boards, the whole dog-and-pony show of blundering into a rural village with scary officials from the capital who almost invariably intimidate the locals into rote performances or frightened, wooden silence. But not in Ghana. Somehow—thanks to some gracious functionaries in air-conditioned offices in a foreign land, on a continent we knew shamefully little about—the people we met were funny and wise and unafraid to speak their minds. There was nothing we were not allowed to see, no hidden agendas, no reminders to "be sure to show Americans our modern infrastructure" or "charming tribal customs."

A whole village works together to pull in the nets outside Accra.

(Above left) Rennik, jacked up on adrenaline and general craziness, finds time to hop in front of the camera to get his picture taken with the elephants. This is a classic Rennik pose. Here he is, middle of the Ghanaian jungle, and he's tweaking like it's rush hour in midtown Manhattan. On one hand, that's the level of dedication we like to see in our assistant producers. On the other hand, this guy is gonna blow a freakin' gasket. Note the throbbing vein in his forehead.

Together with our official guides, we were jostled and bullied by market women, boisterously liquored up with distilled jungle brew, asked to explain (again and again), "What is your mission?" by tribal councils wanting to know—exactly and at great length—who were we, where we came from, and what the hell we were doing in their village. We were treated with affection, generosity, and respect everywhere—by people who'd seldom seen, barely recognized, and could care less about a central authority. And along the way, we saw where civilization as we know it and so much of the life we take for granted began. Rock and roll, blues, rap, reggae, calypso, jazz—their beginnings still recognizable in the traditional music of West Africa. The facial characteristics of so many Americans now poignantly explained. The food unexpectedly delicious—spicy, color-

ful stews, flavors and textural combinations and ingredients that later resonated powerfully when eating "traditional" Southern food. How many of the distinctive features of the white Southern diet—the most treasured culinary notes—are, in fact, black African in origin.

Like so many of the best destinations, Africa is maddening and befuddling to the widely held conceptions and best intentions of the good at heart. It's also devastatingly, humblingly beautiful.

(Opposite right, and above, left and right) Ghana interior: The crew and I wake up to find our camp infested with elephants. This seemed like a good thing, as we'd planned a three-hour safari into the bush in order to capture some pachyderm footage and were now looking at an easy day. Except that the wardens were still asleep, we had no idea what we were doing, and as we soon found out, we were dangerously close to enraging a herd of young males. Note my completely inappropriate shirt, the perfect color to alarm or piss off an elephant.

BEAUTIFUL AND BEFUDDLING, AFRICA SUPPLIES NO EASY ANSWERS.

Todd on the job in an Ashanti village.

(Opposite) Accra: Woman with shea nuts at market. (Above) The Ashanti chief presents me with a kente cloth.

NAMIBIA

In Namibia—a featureless, empty country of dry, wide-open spaces and tidy Teutonic cities, where whites still control most of the arable land and Germans still sit around beer halls and complain about the "help"—answers and conclusions are difficult to find. Are third- or fourth-generation white farmers, trying to scrape a living out of the veldt, necessarily bad? Is the (finally) black-administered government necessarily good? Not for the Topnar people, who were pushed off their hunting grounds and into the desert and left to fend for themselves. Certainly not for the Bushmen—a minority long despised by "black" African tribes—who have been, for centuries, forced out to the margins by more-organized groups, to hunt and forage in the near waterless Kalahari basin. On the other hand, the well-meaning Bushmen fed me the number-one worst thing I've ever put in my mouth: a sand-, fur-, and crap-laden warthog—and its last few inches of semi-cleaned poop chute—which, weeks later, sent me off to an emergency session with a gastroenterologist and a full course of antibiotics. No matter. You spin the wheel long enough, sometimes you come up double zero. It's hard to find easy conclusions about anything in Africa—other than a general sense of wanting to help, and the sinking feeling that many of those who've wanted to "help" in the past have only fucked things up worse. What I know for sure? I liked Ghana and enjoyed it and would urge people to visit. Namibia? Less so.

(Above left) With the Kalahari Bushmen in the Namibian interior. (Above right) The Bushmen get busy with a warthog. (Below) Warthog dinner. What turned out to be the worst meal of my life. Later, the likely cause for a two-week course of antibiotics.

(Above) Yarn for sale at the market. (Below left) The glories of Namibian barbecue. (Below right) The work of daily life in a Topnar village.

(Opposite) **Ostrich-egg omelet, Bushman style: Puncture shell, drain directly onto hot embers, cook extra-well, brush off (some of) the ash, and enjoy.** (This page) **Middle of nowhere in the Kalahari basin: Chris and I have a story conference at a deserted airstrip.**

BEIR

UT

Beirut: Earlier, happier times.

I'm sitting, poolside, watching the airport burning, the last of the jet fuel cooking off like a dying can of Sterno. There's a large black plume of smoke coming from the south of the city—just over the rise, where the most recent airstrikes have been targeting the Shiite neighborhoods and what are, presumably, Hezbollah-associated structures. We missed it the first time they hit the airport. Slept right through it. Woke up in our snug hotel sheets to the news that we wouldn't be making television in Beirut (not the show we came to do, anyway), and that we wouldn't be getting out of here anytime soon.

Any hopes of runway repair followed by a flight out disappeared two nights ago, when we watched from the balcony of my room as missiles, fired from offshore, twinkled brightly for a few long seconds in the air, then dropped in lazy parabolas onto the fuel tanks.

We knew by this time what was happening in the south: Hezbollah rocketing Israel, the Israeli army mobilizing along—and even crossing—

It felt like Miami—with better restaurants. And then . . .

the border, artillery firing, reserves being called up. Frightened visitors from Persian Gulf states and the Lebanese—including our local fixer—had headed for Syria, but the planes had been hitting that route out repeatedly, making the already unattractive option of camera-bearing Americans crossing into that unwelcoming country even less attractive. Exit by sea was out of the question in light of a total naval blockade. We were stuck. The other American guests—at first secure in "this doesn't concern us" and "they won't target us" and "we're just waiting for word" mode—were now visibly worried about themselves.

Everything had begun so beautifully. Our fixer, Lena, was bursting with enthusiasm when she met us at the airport. After months of preproduction, finally we were here! Finally, the American television crew had arrived—to show the world how beautiful her country was, how lovingly restored, how hip and forward-thinking it had become in the years since the bloody civil war. First day of filming, we'd had a sensational early lunch of

The restaurant Le Chef. A lively local haunt with great food.

hummus, kibbe, stewed lamb, and yogurt at Le Chef, a local, family-style joint in a charming neighborhood. The customers at the tables around us in the tiny, worn-looking dining area chattered away in Arabic, French, and English. Stomachs full, my crew and I headed over to Martyr's Square and the Hariri memorial a few blocks away, our fixer and friends pointing out old scars and new construction, trying to explain how much Beirut and Lebanon had changed. They spoke effusively of the calm, the peace, the relative tolerance that had followed the former prime minister's galvanizing assassination. Each smiled and pointed at the giant photographic mural on the memorial's wall of the million-person demonstration that had led to Syria's withdrawal from their country; Ali, our unofficial tough-guy escort, pointed at a tiny dot among the hundreds of thousands in the photo and joked, "That's me!" They were so proud of how far they'd come, how they'd survived, how different and sophisticated Beirut was now. They spoke of all the things they had to show us, the people we had to meet.

Hezbollah drive through a scene we're shooting and Tracey gets it on tape. The precise moment that we first noticed things were going bad.

Significantly, the word "Syria" was still spoken in slightly hushed tones. Speaking too long, too loud, or too harshly of their former occupier could still—it was suggested—get you killed. (An outcome not without precedent.) We walked along the road leading to a cordoned-off area by the St. George Hotel, where Bardot, Monroe, and Kim Philby had once played, back when Beirut was called the Paris of the Orient without a hint of irony. The buildings in the area were still in ruins, the old hotel—under construction when the targeted blast had killed Hariri—still empty. But the Phoenician, across the street, had recently been completely rebuilt, a modern hotel like any other—but they were proud of that, too. Because—like Beirut—it was still there. It was back.

Then, in the blink of an eye, everything went sideways: relaxed smiles froze and disappeared at the sound of automatic weapons firing randomly in the air from a nearby neighborhood. And fireworks . . . Then cars, a few of them, with teenage kids and adults, some leaning out the windows and

The news only got worse. And worse.

waving Hezbollah flags and flashing the V-for-Victory sign, celebrating what we were told—after a few quick cell phone calls—was the grabbing of two Israeli soldiers. Our fixer, a Sunni; Ali, a Shiite; and "Marwan," a Christian, who'd just minutes ago been pointing proudly at the mural—all three looked down in embarrassment, a look of sorrow, shame, and then resignation on their faces. Someone bitterly muttered, "Assholes." They knew right away what was going to happen next.

Not that that stopped the party—not initially, anyway. Beirutis like to tell you (true or not) that they partied right through the civil war. That it wasn't "cool" to seek shelter during an airstrike. That we "shouldn't worry. All the nightclubs have their own generators." That night, we continued to shoot (and drink heavily) at the opening party for the newly relocated Sky Bar, a rooftop nightclub with a view of the Med. Moneyed Beirutis—all of them, it seemed, young, sexy, and ridiculously beautiful, drank vodka and Red Bull, and swayed (if not exactly danced) while Israeli jets flew menac-

With smoke pouring from the bombed-out airport, it became clear that our way home was closed off.

ingly low overhead. Were it not for the warplanes, it could have been Los Angeles—or South Beach.

But any pretense that the "party never stops in Beirut" was gone by the next morning when the airport was hit, for the first of many times. A naval blockade precluded any escape by boat. For those who could, the road to Damascus was the only option, and Lena—and Ali—urged us to take it. But the network and our production company were reluctant to sign off on what even then seemed a dodgy undertaking.

We found ourselves in my room, watching them hit the airport again: me; camera people Tracey, Todd, and Jerry; field producer Diane; our fixer—and Ali. Our fixer, at the urging of her father in Syria, tearfully agreed to join him there. Our driver—an hour earlier waiting outside, gassed up and ready to go—disappeared. Ali alone remained; he refused to leave us. "I am with you," he said. But after observing numerous calls to and from his family in South Beirut, and seeing the way he was working the prayer beads

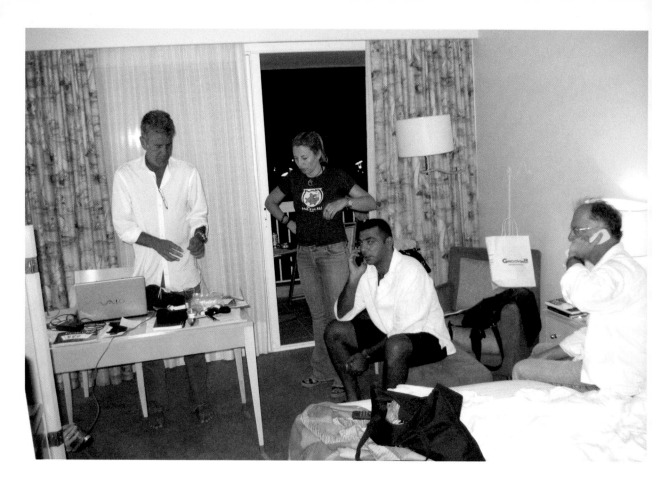

The airport has just been hit again—not far from our window. And we're calling loved ones, telling them we don't know how we're getting home, or when, but not to worry. That's our Shiite bodyguard, Ali, in center of the room. He refused to leave us—even though his neighborhood was being bombed. We had to beg him to join his family.

between his fingers, the sword tattoo on his arm flexing and unflexing nervously, we insisted he join them. (We later heard his house was flattened.) We were left to ourselves, emptying my minibar and trying to keep a stiff upper lip, telling stupid jokes, while the orange glow from the airport flared and subsided and finally died.

After a series of very worried calls from the States, we are told to stand by for "The Cleaner," a "security expert," "like the Harvey Keitel guy in *Pulp Fiction*," the man who will "get us out," take us to a "safe house," a "secure location," "exfiltrate us" to safety. We are told to be packed, to be ready. To expect a call from "Mr. Wolf."

Three A.M. and I get the call. Shortly after, I meet the man in the lobby. I'd been picturing an ex–Green Beret—an aging Dolph Lundgren type with a thick neck, steel-gray eyes, a tattoo saying HE WHO DARES WINS— all business and mysterious past. Then a midnight drive in a flatbed truck— maybe hidden under a tarp. Bribes at the border . . . a next-day rendezvous

Jerry, Todd, and Tracey. Their expressions say everything.

with a blacked-out helicopter . . . Instead, the man I meet is a short, nebbishy type who looks like someone you'd meet at an office-supply convention. He has two cars out front: his, and another driven by a woman associate. We load out quickly and race through empty streets, blowing through traffic lights, last-minute turns, no directionals, to the other side of town, to Le Royale, a mammoth hotel on a hill in the Christian section—fairly close to the American embassy. This—as it turns out—will be our home for the next week.

Nearly a week later: They've brought in a polka band to play in the dining room of the "Mexican"-themed restaurant at Le Royale. Outside, on the pool deck, though the bar is unattended, where the bottles were they keep the radio cranked up to drown out the sounds of bombing—so as not to scare the kiddies. These days, we wake up to molar-vibrating percussions and go to sleep to distant thunder. Afternoons, we watch as Beirut is dismantled, bit by bit. First the sound of unseen jets flying overhead. Then

Evacuees wait for a way out.

silence. Then a *boom*! Then a distant plume of smoke. Black, brown, white
. . . the whole city south of us slowly growing more indistinct in the mid-
day light under a constant smoglike haze.

We're by the pool a lot. We sit. We play cards. We tell the same half-
hearted dick jokes. But by now, that's all that keeps us from going crazy or
bursting into tears. Our irregular "intel" (Mr. Wolf's favorite word) consists
of printed analysis from a faraway corporate security company (useless spec-
ulation), BBC news (pretty good), local TV (excellent—though in Arabic)
the Hezbollah Channel (scary), Sky News (shockingly up-to-date and thorough), "Some Guy from the Pool" (almost always on target—he accurately
predicts locations and times of airstrikes and seems to know which countries' citizens are getting out and when), "Somebody's Mom Back in the
States" (excellent source) and Mr. Wolf's printouts from the AOL News
website (always discouraging). We call the embassy day after day and get
no response. Nothing. Officially—after days of war—the State

Citizen.

Department's advice is to visit their website. Which contains nothing of use.

We watch the city we'd barely begun to know, and yet already started to love, destroyed—seemingly without sense or reason. We watch Blackhawk helicopters fly in and out of the embassy compound and hear panicked rumors that they're evacuating the ambassador (false) and "non-essential personnel" (true, I believe). Around the pool, the increasingly frustrated "guests," mostly Lebanese Americans, exchange rumors and information gleaned from never-ending cell phone conversations with we-don't-know-who: relatives in the south, friends back in America, people who've already made it out. Friends who've spoken to their congressman. Guys who work at CNN . . . the list goes on. The news maddening, incomplete, incorrect—alternately hopeful, terrifying, and dismaying.

The hotel empties and fills and empties again.

We hear:

"The Italians got out!"

Diane, as we try and figure out how we're going to get past Lebanese security forces and the outer security cordon. People were passing out from heatstroke in the shadeless street, children and babies crying, seemingly no one in charge. Confusion reigned—until we finally made it into the custody of the Marines.

"The fucking *Romanians* got out!"

"The French are gone!"

What is clear—as far as we're concerned—from *all* sources is that there is no official, announced plan. No real advice, or information, or public exit strategy or timetable. The news clip of President Bush, chawing open-mouthed on a buttered roll, then grabbing at another while Tony Blair tries to get him to focus on Lebanon, plays over and over on the TV, crushing our spirits and dampening hope with every glassy-eyed mouthful. He seems intent on enjoying his food; Lebanon a tiny, annoying blip on an otherwise blank screen. I can't tell you how depressing that innocuous bit of footage is to watch. That one innocent, momentary preoccupation with a roll has an effect on us that's out of all proportion. We're looking for signs. And this—sadly—is all we have.

And every day we hear worse. Cell phone towers, power stations, land-lines are being targeted, says Mr. Wolf. And we're frankly terrified of the

Marines and a CNN crew wait for more evacuees.

seemingly imminent moment when we can no longer stay in touch with the outside world, make or receive calls to the States—or more important, be notified by the embassy (should that ever happen). They've run out of bread and food in downtown stores.

And yet, here, still safe and fed and liquored-up in Bizarro World, we sit by the pool and watch the war. And wait, impotently—shame-facedly. As the hotel empties again—and only a few of us are left. Expectations fade and then die. Just bitterness and a sense of disgust remain. What to expect anymore? One hopes only for the little things: that they'll fire up the pizza oven today. That they'll open the bar early. That we might just maybe get an English-language newspaper or mag-azine—or even a French one.

A few miles away, of course, hopes are similarly downscaled—yet far, far more urgent:

We are evacuated onto an LCU.

Will there be bread?

Will there be water?

Will the power come back on?

Is my family okay?

Will I die today?

They've hit the little lighthouse by the port. While insisting that the Lebanese government do "something" about Hezbollah, the Israelis have shelled an army base, the main bridges and roads, even (says "Some Guy from the Pool") the last roads out to Syria. An end or even a pause in the attacks is way too much for any of us to hope for. Of that we are certain. And certainty—however terrible the truth—is something we cling to. It's uncertainty that's the enemy, the thing we know will make us all crazy.

In the end, we are among the lucky ones. The privileged, the fortunate, the relatively untouched. Unlike the Lebanese Americans who make it out, we don't leave homes and loved ones behind; we will get out and return to

Diane with crew members on the USS *Nashville*.

business as usual. To unbroken homes, intact families, friends, and jobs. After a hideously disorganized clusterfuck at the eventual "assembly point"—a barely controlled mob scene of fainting old people, crying babies, desperate families waving pink and white slips of paper, trying to get the attention of a few understaffed, underprepared, and seemingly annoyed embassy personnel in baseball caps and casual clothes—we are put in the care of the sailors and Marines of the USS *Nashville*—who've hauled ass from Jordan on short notice. They perform brilliantly. The moment we pass through the last checkpoint into their control, all are treated with a kindness and humanity we can scarcely believe. Squared away, efficient, organized, and caringly sensitive, the Marines break the crowd into sensibly spaced groups, give them shade and water, lead them single file to an open-ended landing craft at the water's edge. They carry babies, children, heatstroke victims, luggage. They are soft-spoken, casually friendly. They give out treats and fruit and water. They reassure us with their ease and professionalism.

Crossing the Mediterranean on the USS *Nashville*. Later, at an event for the Marine Corps—to whom I am eternally and deeply grateful—I was told that the ship is commonly referred to in the ranks as the "Trashville." She was beautiful to me.

On the flight deck of the *Nashville* they've set up a refugee camp. I wake up on my folding cot and look around. With every group of traumatized evacuees—with every family, every group of children, there's a Marine or two, chatting, exchanging stories, listening. They open their ship to us. They look so young. All of them. None looks over seventeen. "Where you from?" one asks me. I say New York—and he tells me, "I ain't ever been there. I'd like to." His friends agree. They've never seen New York either. The mess serves tuna noodle casserole and mac-and-cheese and corn dogs. A sailor or Marine in a bright green dragon suit entertains children. We are kept informed. We are reassured. We are spoken to like adults. On the smoking deck, a Marine shows off a Reuters cover photo—taken only a few hours earlier—of himself, nuzzling two babies as he carries them through the surf to the landing craft. His buddies are razzing him, busting his balls for how intolerably big-headed he's going to be now that he's "famous." He looks at the picture and says, "You don't know what it felt like, man." His eyes well up.

On the plane home from Cyprus after ten days in Beirut. I was thoroughly discouraged, filled with shame, and didn't have much hope left for the world.

The last group from the beach is unloaded from the landing craft into the belly of the *Nashville*, and we're off to Cyprus. Two battleships—including the USS *Cole*—escorting us. A Lebanon I never got to know, a Beirut I didn't get to show the world disappears slowly over the horizon—a beautiful dream turned nightmare. It's not what I saw happen in Beirut that I feel like talking about—though that's what I'm doing, isn't it? It's not about what happened to me that remains an unfinished show, a not fully fleshed out story, or even a particularly interesting one. It feels shameful even writing this. It's the story I didn't get to tell. The Beirut I saw for two short days. The possibilities. The hope. Now only a dream.

EURO

PE

ICELAND

If you pushed the state of Maine out into the ocean, covered it with subarctic tundra, and brought the entire populace of St. Paul, Minnesota, there to bore one another to death, you'd have Iceland. Iceland . . . Iceland . . . Iceland . . . A good show—though not an entirely happy experience. What is there to do in Iceland but drink, soak in a fucking hot spring or a steam bath or a lagoon, and then drink again? Now factor in a cuisine rooted in limited local resources and, seemingly, a wide streak of the perverse. The notoriously stinky fermented shark was, in fact, the second-worst thing I've ever put in my mouth. I did like the local chefs, who do a lot with a little and cook very, very well. But I got the impression they'd rather be elsewhere. Who wouldn't?

Iceland in winter.
The blizzard begins.

LOVELY, YES, BUT POSSIBLY THE MOST BORING PLACE ON EARTH.

(Above and below) Chris and I take a break from shooting in an underground ice cave to enjoy a glass of Black Death. (Opposite) Iceland, the freaking middle of nowhere. Blistering cold. Miles of featureless snow. An angry host. Even the dogs were bored. Now *that's* quality television!

Get drunk. Soak in hot lagoon. Get drunk again. Here I am in the Blue Lagoon, post-bender. My head feels like a family of angry bonobo apes has been crapping in it. (Opposite) Traditional Icelandic holiday treats. Testicle terrine—marinated in lactic acid. Blood sausage—marinated in lactic acid. Rotten shark. Marinated in lactic acid. The smell alone could drop a charging rhino (or Rachael Ray) in its tracks from fifty yards. And the taste? Beyond imagining. The cold sheep head was the best part.

A true Irish pub: one of the happier places on earth.

IRELAND

There are few places I'm more comfortable than a really good Irish pub. A true, properly poured pint of Guinness (available nowhere but Ireland, to my mind) snuggles into the hand like another appendage. The golden light through streaked windows, the sound of Irish barroom conversation, a football game on a distant screen . . . maybe a few notes from a trio of musicians, seated at a nearby table.

Like a lot of New Yorkers, I'm incorrigible in my republican sympathies—however distasteful I might have found the Provos. These leanings were only reinforced in Belfast, where the Protestants' wall murals loudly proclaim their complete tone-deafness to good public relations. How can you sell your position to the world when your advertisements all contain hooded gunmen, blood-red hands, and anonymous, fascistic imagery interchangeable with that of Hussein-era Iraq, Ceauşescu's Romania, Mano Blanco El Salvador, Dirty War Argentina? To the outsider, Protestant Belfast looks scary. Catholic Belfast, by contrast, shrewdly depicts itself as beleaguered, martyred, devout. In its murals, the fallen, gunmen and victims alike, are smiling, gentle-looking, beatific.

That said, I love Belfast, as I love Dublin, and Cork, and everywhere else I've

been in this maddening and maddeningly beautiful country. I never have any idea whether I'm talking to a Catholic or a Prot and couldn't care less. The murals and the history seem completely divorced from the people I've met.

Plus the food. Good food in Ireland? Yes! Absolutely! On top of the glories of the Irish breakfast—a life-affirming and Guinness-complementing mess of bacon, sausage, fried eggs, black pudding, and tomato—Ireland has beautiful lamb, fish, cheeses . . . and a new generation of cooks who know what to do with them.

(Opposite) **County Cork: No baby pigs were hurt or killed during the making of this program.** (Above) **The genius of the Irish breakfast, the culmination of thousands of years of tradition in a place that knows something about fighting off brain-melting hangovers.**

Public relations, Belfast-style. (Above left) The Republican hero, the beatific-looking Bobby Sands. (Above right and below) Protestant murals.

(Above) Todd hitches a ride. (Below, left and right) County Cork: Road bowling. Bets are made. A heavy iron ball gets pitched down a country road—through traffic. Mayhem and fun ensue!

PARIS

Mother Europe. My mother, anyway.

The Paris episode was the very first one we filmed. The idea being that we'd avoid the Eiffel Tower, the Louvre, the Arc de Triomphe, and any and all fine-dining restaurants, concentrating instead on the kind of everyday French that the French themselves take for granted: the little bistros, the morning meat market, a croissant for breakfast, good bread, an ordinary *sandwiche jambon* at an ordinary café.

True, what France thinks is great about itself is no longer so great. Its haute cuisine is increasingly eclipsed and irrelevant. Its film industry, a welfare state; its motto, "Liberté, égalité, fraternité," a joke—as outdated, sadly, as our "Give us your tired, your poor, your huddled masses . . . " But waking up in Paris and walking the streets of Saint-Germain-des-Prés, finding yourself a grilled kidney or a humble plate of stewed veal, knocking back an early-morning calvados with bloodstained meat cutters at Rungis, waiting on line for the *pain raisins* to come out of the oven at the pâtisserie—or a late-afternoon pastis, or a few belon oysters from a rubber-booted shucker—it brings back why we owe a debt to France, not just every time we pick up a knife, but pretty much all the time.

The cranky, contentious, know-it-all, cheese-eating surrender monkeys, after all,

The Oscar Wilde Suite at L'Hotel. This was the very first episode of the series, and I'm contemplating, no doubt, what it all means.

largely underwrote our struggle for independence—bankrupting themselves in the process. They did give us the Statue of Liberty. And our films and popular entertainment would probably still be stuck in dumb-ass had not Truffaut, Godard, Chabrol, et al. reminded us what was great about Ford, Hawks, and Hitchcock and moved the language of film in new, gorgeously black-and-white directions. Sometimes it takes the French—always the crank at the party—to remind us what's fucked up about ourselves (Iraq) and what's great (jazz, underground comix, Maine lobster, Idaho potatoes). The show we did in Paris was payback in troubled, Francophobic times—a useful reminder, I hope, of what's truly great and glorious, in a timeless way, about France.

(Above) The wine cellar at Chez Denise. The skulls, presumably, are not those of earlier customers. (Opposite) Absinthe.

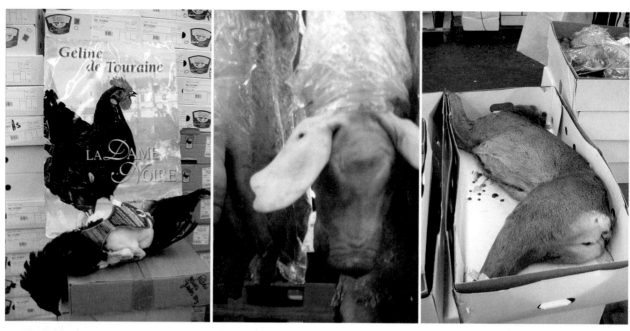

(Above left and center) Rungis Market. (Above right) Why Christmas will be a little late this year. (Below) The butchers' café at Rungis Market. These guys are into their second bottle of wine and their third calvados—and it's only seven in the morning! I love France.

(Above) Rungis Market. (Below) After missing the shot, Tracey and Chris try to convince me to "do it again."

SICILY

The Sicily show was fucked up from the get-go. Most maddening was that, trapped in a hopelessly botched, badly planned itinerary—and shepherded about by a constantly changing team of shifty characters—we could only look out at what might have been. An outrageously beautiful country full of great food and great people . . . Pantelleria, easily one of the most gorgeous places on earth, with its centuries-old Arab-style *dammusi*, white-domed homes set among sharp-edged black lava . . . blue skies, the wind from Africa around us. And we mostly missed it. The one great moment was an accident: a crude lunch of spaghetti in red

sauce, grilled fish, and some rough home-made wine with a group of caper farmers. Palermo, Lampedusa, Taormina, Catania? A procession of cobbled-together scenes: me drinking piña coladas on a beach . . . talking movies with last-minute interviewee Vincenzo Tripodo in front of the unexpected JumboTron at the ancient amphithe-

ater . . . a stone-cold, butt-ugly stunt lunch by the crater at Etna . . . an ill-considered jump from a high cliff . . . breakfast with the president (why?) . . . bogus pizza . . . three hours of watching my crew cheese up from a squid boat—all for nothing, nothing, nothing. Like Peter Fonda said to Dennis Hopper in *Easy Rider*: "We blew it."

Pantelleria: The crew sits down with our hosts at a caper farm. I admit that I had very low expectations for this scene. Picking capers didn't sound fun or dramatic, and the episode as a whole had been going very badly. But, as is so often the case, it's the people who make the meal. These farmers were great—funny, warm, good cooks, and really good company. It was one of those happy accidents, an unexpected, perfect confluence of events where everything—people, landscape, food, and timing—all came together. In one eerily wonderful moment, I realized that though I don't speak Italian, I understood every word my hosts were saying. Fucking magic!

SWEDEN

Sweden was one long Abba joke. Not a good sign. Abba jokes are like dick jokes—too many of them is an indicator that things aren't going well. The food was surprisingly good, but hilariously funny or passionate the Swedes ain't. It's neat, it's clean, orderly, tolerant . . . It works . . . There's very little crime . . . Everybody's pretty damned content. Not my kind of place at all.

Above the arctic circle, Todd contemplates the prospect of another night in our frigid *laavu*.

(Above) Lapland: "Reindeer. It's what's for dinner. And lunch." Waiting for dinner in a *laavu*—Swedish for "a freezing, smoke-filled tent"— with a Sami, one of the indigenous reindeer-herding people. Later, when bunking with Todd, Jerry, and Chris, the fire in our heater kicked out. I woke up, nearly hypothermic, my crew's delirious moans warning me that death was near. I alone ventured out into the snow to gather wood. Using local currency for kindling, I was able to restart the fire—thus saving all our lives. Thankfully, as a smoker, I had a lighter on me. (Below) Chris, Jerry, Todd, and I thaw out in the hot tub after a night on the tundra.

SWEDEN: A NICE PLACE WHERE NOTHING BAD HAPPENS. AND NOTHING ESPECIALLY GOOD, EITHER.

(Above) Stockholm is a great "chef and cook" city, with a vibrant after-work culinary culture of recognizable "types." Any American or French chef would feel immediately at home here. But I'm not usually a fan of tidy European cities—especially ones where everything works predictably and there are few enlivening social problems. (Below) With members of the Stubborn MC motorcycle club. In Sweden even the bikers are nice.

NORT
AME

H
RICA

UNITED STATES

I used to look at America as New York, L.A., San Francisco, that place in Florida where New Yorkers go to die on the beach—and the "flyover": all that stuff in between. And it was easy, seeing the country on numerous book tours, to find supporting evidence for that wrongheaded view. Standing at the window in your hotel room in Houston, or Denver, or Minneapolis, or Detroit, looking out at a mind-numbing, soul-grinding stretch of the same replicated businesses—Denny's, Victoria's Secret, the Gap, McDonald's, Borders, Starbucks, Macaroni Grill, Chili's, on and on, stretching to the horizon toward a tiny distant city of narrow glass boxes—it's easy to think, That's all there is.

Then, one time, looking down from a plane somewhere over Colorado, I noticed, "Hey! There really are 'purple mountains'! There really is a 'fruited plain'!" Little by little, one by one, the people I met and the things I saw began to chip away at my preconceptions. Once I began looking at my own country as I would a foreign land, showing Cleveland, for instance, the same respect for local language, customs, and practices not my own that I instinctively gave Vietnam, it was easy to find lots to admire, to be intrigued by, and to love.

With the sheriff of
Eagle Pass, Texas.

NY/LA

New York and L.A. present an intriguing problem to would-be makers of quality television entertainment: How to do an hour of food/travel television without repeating what every other travel-and-food-show fucktard host has already done? How to avoid the usual tropes, clichés, destinations? In our case, we solved our crisis of inspiration in time-honored fashion: We ripped off other artists. Deciding that the New York show would pay homage to *Taxi Driver*, we shot an hour mostly on places that chefs eat after work. In L.A., we tried to emulate the late-era Friedkin look—all orangey and working-class, oil rigs and freeways, dying palms and everything but Hollywood. The resulting show was, to the limits of our ability, about the people who actually work in L.A.—as opposed to, say, the VP Development of a studio. It's too easy to make the usual jokes about the differences between the East Coast and the West Coast, so we concentrated instead on striving ethnic communities, little hole-in-the-wall joints, the marginal and marginalized. The last scene, which featured my old friend and chef Sam—now a meat-delivery guy in the Valley—was about redemption through work. As Sam was fresh out of the slammer, we had to fight like demons to get it past the censors, who thought it was "off brand." I think it was right on point: It's not what's

"You talkin' to me? You talkin' to me?" From our disturbingly dark New York show. An exploration of the New York that chefs enjoy, after hours, but also an homage to *Taxi Driver*, complete with psychotic ramblings and guns. Now there's a theme we didn't tell the network about!

different about New York and L.A.; it's what's the same. The same enormous stratum of people waking up each day and heading off to work at jobs that can hardly be described as their "dream." The L.A. show was about doing the best you can.

(Opposite) "Here's a great idea! We'll send Tony to train with the LAPD Hawthorne Division SWAT team!" Okay . . . maybe not. But it was a lot of fun for me—especially the live-fire exercise with "hostage situation." (Above) Los Angeles: With Tracey and mariachis in my Delta 88 Royale—on the way to the *birreria*.

(Above) Los Angeles: At Philippe's with the L.A. Derby Dolls. Some very dangerous women. (Opposite) Enjoying an afternoon cruise in the city that invented road rage.

LAS VEGAS

Our Vegas show became a crude rip-off of *Fear and Loathing in Las Vegas*—one of my favorite books and films. And I think, on balance, we did it pretty well. What the network thought, seeing me and my friend and nemesis, author Michael Ruhlman, careening around the desert in a rented vintage Caddy, drinking our way through an article I was writing for *Gourmet* on celebrity-chef outposts, I have no idea. It was an early effort, and they were, no doubt, horrified by the appearance of hired midgets, showgirls, a Sammy Davis Jr. imitator—and a cameo appearance by cameraman Todd Liebler as Carmen, the deaf, one-eyed accordion-playing hitchhiker. I'm very proud of the episode—thanks in great part to the fearsome, quasi-psychedelic editing of Chris Martinez.

Michael Ruhlman, playing the part of Dr. Gonzo, catches some sun in the front seat of the Red Shark.

(Above left) A flying Elvis. His wrist camera malfunctioned and I had to jump twice. (Above right) Chris, Tracey, and I show off our bruises after a tension-breaking paintball match. It's only fun until someone loses an eye! (Below) The cast and crew of the Vegas shoot, outside the sleazy motel room we rented for a scene: midgets, showgirls, hustlers—and a motorcycle gang that just happened to be there.

(Above) At the Neon Sign Graveyard, off Decatur Boulevard. The last stop for the Las Vegas of Dino, Frank, and Bugsy Siegel.
(Below) Degenerate gambler Nari Kye, on the one other occasion we let her out of the office. I'm trying to concentrate on my deep-fried Twinkies and Oreos. She, no doubt, is trying to convince the crew that betting, drinking, and karaoke are in order.

BIKERS, SHOWGIRLS, DWARFS: THE VEGAS EPISODE WAS OUR TRIBUTE TO HUNTER S. THOMPSON'S TWISTED, APOCALYPTIC MASTERPIECE.

Yes, they surf in
Cleveland. In the middle
of winter. On a lake.

CLEVELAND

Cleveland, of all places, gave us one of the best shows we've ever done. The city's faded, postindustrial Rust Belt glory—its steel mills, railroad bridges, once-magnificent skyline—is beautiful to me. And the people who are scratching out a living there making good food seem all the more heroic when you consider the city's population is half what it was in the 1950s.

Among its other heroes is the sainted Harvey Pekar, whose cranky, brilliant chronicle-in-comics of his life in the crumbling Midwest has become an institution in American letters—now made famous by the movie *American Splendor*. Trudging with Pekar—his arm in a sling after a nasty fall—through the snow-covered streets of Cleveland, past rows of modest houses built for workers in now-shuttered mills, or touring a defunct Twinkie plant that's being reborn, miraculously, as a used bookstore, you can feel America stretching away endlessly in every direction. Still a country of visionaries and strivers.

FRUCTOSE
SYRUP

At the defunct Twinkie factory.
Twenty years later—and the
creamy filling is still fresh!
(Opposite) Cleveland's poet
laureate, its Homer: *American
Splendor's* Harvey Pekar.

The last of the steel mills . . .
(Opposite) The closed-down
Westinghouse plant, which at its
peak employed some eight
thousand workers.

(Above) With Marky Ramone at the Rock and Roll Hall of Fame.
(Below left) Diane does a 3-Way! At Skyline Chili. (Below right) Chef Michael Symon shows us his skin art.
(Opposite) Michael Ruhlman and I butcher some boutique hog for cassoulet and charcuterie.

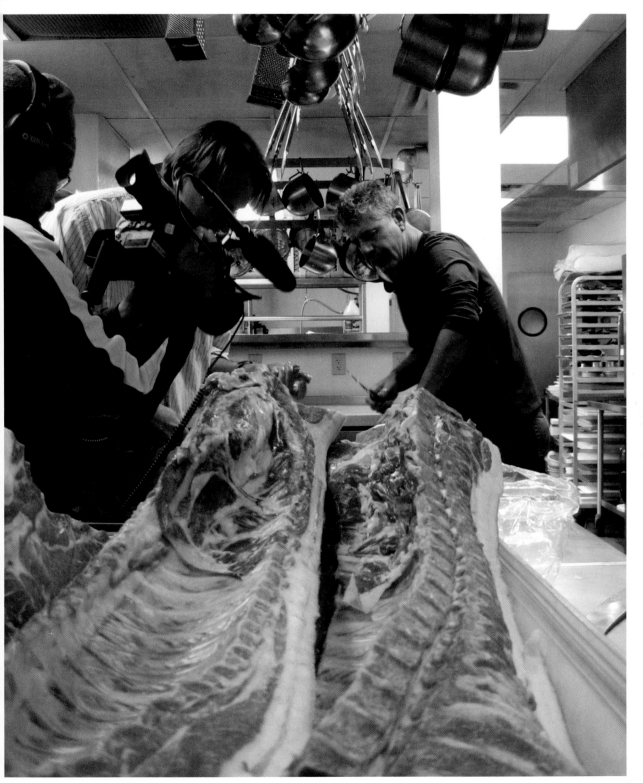

PACIFIC NORTHWEST

From my vantage point in Manhattan, I tend to look at Seattle and Portland more or less the way J. Edgar Hoover looked at the Merry Pranksters: as an enclave of unwashed hemp fetishists, privileged layabouts, and creeping vegetarianism. Yet I love those towns. I insisted we make a show in Portland after numerous book-flogging jaunts there, having discovered the remarkable subculture of obsessive culinarians, artisanal producers, mushroom wranglers, pizza makers, and cooks—many of them heavily inked, and nearly all of them wildly enthusiastic. Seattle, a city known for having plenty of things I hate (hippies, skater boys in dreadlocks, ferries, and serial killers) and things I care little about (salmon, organics, alt-rock bands), also has one of the most vibrant food cultures in America—and, perhaps as important, the single greatest food-serving and -producing establishment on the West Coast: Armandino Batali's tiny and heroic sandwich and sausage shop, Salumi. Seattle has more authentic French food than Los Angeles, more and better cheese than Wisconsin, fresher and more exciting seafood than New York. People are focused on food—quality food—in our Pacific Northwest, and that always makes a place worth visiting.

Portland: White clam
pizza at Apizza Scholls.

(Opposite) Seattle: Mario Batali's aunt Izzy makes gnocchi in the window of Salumi. (Above) Working the sandwich counter at Salumi.

Seattle.

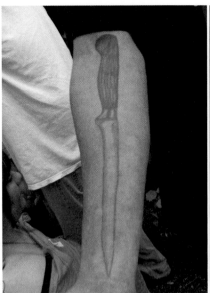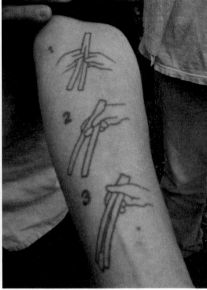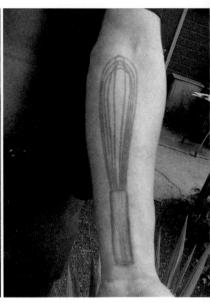

(Above and below) Portland: We put the word out that we wanted chefs and cooks with food- or cooking-related skin art. These guys showed up. (Opposite) My humble contribution.

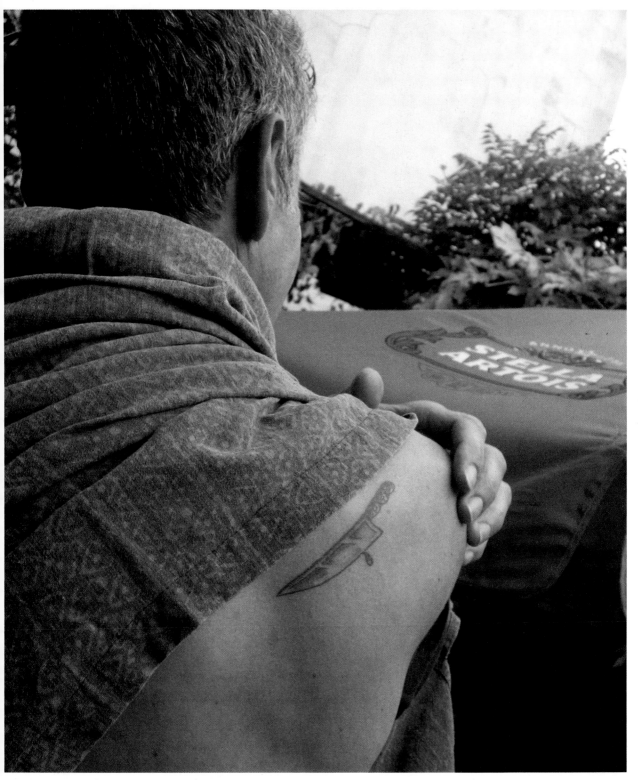

(Opposite) Portland: Sharing a drink with author Chuck Palahniuk at Velveteria, the black-velvet-painting museum. (Above left) Crab at Pike's Market. (Above right) Digging for geoduck in Shelton, Washington. No dick jokes, please. (Below) These highly trained, well-educated professionals just can't seem to get their minds out of the gutter.

Seal hunting with the Inuit. "Without the seal, we would die," said my guide.

QUEBEC

Our Mysterious Brothers to the North, the Canadians, provided a great time and, I think, a great show. Actually, fuck the Canadians: The Quebecois provided a great time and a great show. What is it about cantankerous, nationalistic, potentially violent, dialect-speaking peoples that I find so appealing? I admire a strong sense of distinct identity—of "otherness," I suppose. Clearly, as with the Basque, the Belfast Irish, and the Sicilians of Pantelleria, I identify with their pugnacity and stubborn pride. Or maybe it's just that they always seem to have the best food. On a shoot at Montreal's indispensable Au Pied du Cochon, Martin Picard, the foie gras–crazed lunatic of a chef, told his cooks, "Keep feeding him . . . and stop when he dies." These are my kind of people.

But it was the Inuit of Inukjuak, a long, scary-ass flight in an ice-encrusted puddle jumper to the way-north, who brought us one of those life-changing "Golden Moments." The bleak, frozen wasteland of the Hudson Bay—all steel gray, freezing whiteout snows and emptiness, where nothing grows; a place as far from the riotous colors and varied flavors of my beloved Asia as can be—provided everything we hope for and aspire to in our hungry travels. The ice still melting off our temporarily cold-paralyzed cameras; a dead seal ripped open on a kitchen floor. A family gathered to eat. The bright, unexpected red of the animal's raw interior practically burning our eyes. In a small, warm place—surrounded by thousands of miles of stinging, bone-aching cold, our hosts licking blood from their fingers—we found all those things that others, back home in comfortable apartments, only write about and talk about and hope for in the abstract. Love, family, meaning. Everything stands on its head—everything you believe is wrong.

(Above) Montreal: Where foie gras comes from. (Right) Montreal: Duck-processing plant.

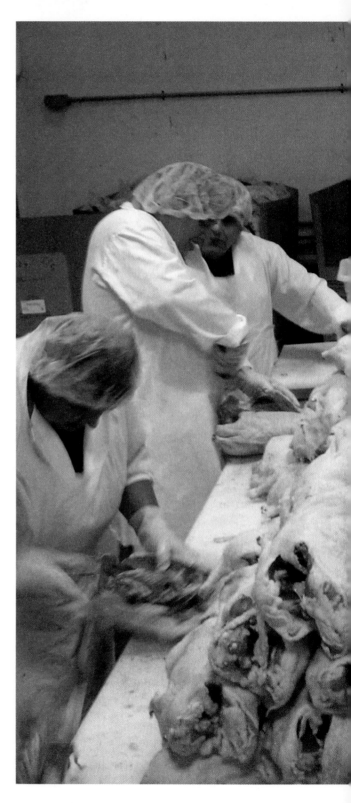

Montreal: At Au Pied de Cochon, where rogue chef Martin Picard tried to kill me with food. Fourteen courses of such lite fare as *poutine* with foie gras, foie gras tart, foie gras burger, cassoulet, foie gras–stuffed pig's foot, and, too much of a good thing being not enough, the pièce de résistance: a maple-glazed pig's head with gilded snout.

(Opposite) Inukjuak: Raw seal on the kitchen floor with my Inuit hosts. (Above) Grandma offers me an eyeball. (Below) Seal: It's not just for breakfast anymore.

MEXICO/TEXAS

Texas, a state New Yorkers almost instinctively dismiss as a place where the "stupids" live, offers a particularly delightful variety of comeuppances to those who underestimate her. I have found out the hard way that in Texas, letting you know—slooowwwly—that you're the stupidest person in the room is something of an art form, and is considered local sport. Few in Texas will tell you right up front that you're a dumb-ass. That would be too easy for you. They let you find that out for yourself.

In a show exploring the tortured, symbiotic relationship between Mexican immigrants and their sometime employers to the north, I found far more tolerance than in areas less affected by the issue. I got a tremendous amount of angry mail on that episode—most

The Rio Grande, the traditional border that mostly fails to separate the U.S. and Mexico.

of it from places like Maine, where you'd be hard-pressed to find a Mexican of any kind, let alone an illegal one. Where Texans and Mexicans live side by side, just about everybody I met was superbly bilingual (something you can't say about New Yorkers) and undogmatic. Where it matters, there is an appreciation of all things Mexican—the food, music, and people—that comes, perhaps, with having Mexico so close. So much of what's good about Texas is, in fact, from south of the border. And no one knows that better than Texans. I'll never forget the sheriff of Eagle Pass, squinting out across the Rio Grande from under his ten-gallon hat—every inch the aging cowboy hero—wondering what this "wall they were thinking of building" was all about.

Monster Jeep riding along
the Tex-Mex border.

(Above) I learned to ride a motorcycle just for this scene. And don't think I wasn't nervous about damaging this beautiful hunk of German machinery. (Below) When in Texas, buy boots. I'm asking for whatever they think Bobby Flay might wear on a first date.

SOUT
AME

H
RICA

ARGENTINA

I've seen a lot of glaciers in recent years: in Iceland, New Zealand, Yunnan Province in China. But approaching the glacier in Calafate, in southern Patagonia—nearly at the end of the world—I felt less like a tourist marveling at a wonder of nature than like Ahab, staring into the eyes of the White Whale. I saw—or sensed, in a deeply upsetting way—my own death. In the massive, building-sized hunks of ice that dropped periodically from that endlessly creeping wall, I felt for the first time the inevitability of it all, the unquestionable power of forces bigger than me—or anyone I could reach on the phone. The blocks of ice would send a booming *crack* echoing through the air as they broke free—then a huge splash as they plunged into the water, and a terrifyingly deep explosion as they hit

Patagonia: "Gauchos on Ice, Part II." Me and the crew—with drunken gauchos in the rear—try to pick our way off the ice. As we had all come right from a horseback scene, we were wearing crampons on our cowboy boots—not the most sensible footwear.

bottom. A moment later, scary, unnaturally blue chunks would appear, floating on the surface—all that was left of the event.

After a walk on the glacier itself with some drunken gaucho pals (a scene we jokingly referred to as "Gauchos on Ice"), we pulled away in a boat, the inconceivable mass of the ice cliffs growing smaller in the distance—and I felt myself talking to the thing, to the glacier itself: "Not this time. Not yet. But I'll be seeing you. Maybe from under the wheels of a car, or a hospital bed. A bathroom floor, or a plunging plane . . . I don't know. But I will surely see you again."

Perhaps it was this brush with the Infinite that sharpened the pleasures of Buenos Aires, one of the world's more vibrant cities. All you need to know about B.A. is that the Ramones are (still) as big there as the Rolling Stones ever were. Like post-Franco Spain, it's a place happy to be alive—hip, smart, and a new destination for savvy travelers. Where being smart or funny was, not too long ago, dangerous to one's health, people take particular pleasure in the good things of life.

Buenos Aires: Street food. The name
translates as "chasing the cow."

(Above) Living out my old Sergio Leone fantasy in Patagonia. Give me a good horse, a few dogs, and a couple hundred miles of grassland, and I'm Charles Bronson in *Once Upon a Time in the West*. (Below) Buenos Aires's ferias (open-air markets) sell everything from traditional crafts to used furniture—as well as some of the city's best food.

(Above) Buenos Aires: Mise en place. (Below) Buenos Aires: The "villas," low-income city-states within a state.

Preparing for a party of five thousand in Calafate. Is it in poor taste to remark that I was reminded of early Christian martyrs?

São Paulo: At Chez Claudia.
Cachaça brings people
together.

BRAZIL

Why do I love—immediately—some places and not others? It's easy to understand why Rio and Bahia have instant appeal, but why Peru, or Buenos Aires? Unspoiled natural beauty and magnificent vistas generally leave me feeling, frankly, a little bored and wishing someone would start a knife fight or something. So why did Patagonia grab hold of me?

São Paulo is perhaps easier to understand. Though it's crowded, polluted, and mostly ugly, I have friends there, a group of smart, funny, talented women who have repeatedly shown me a side of their city I might never otherwise have seen. The show we did there is reflective of that; it's mostly about people and the uniquely Paulista attitude of work hard, hustle hard, then relax and have fun with abandon.

(Opposite) Waiting for a helicopter ride. (Above) Walking in B.A. (Below left) Rennik and Todd reenact an old favorite scene from *The Naked Chef*. (Below right) Pineapple vendor.

The two faces of Brazil: on one hand, some of the most breathtaking beaches and jungles on earth . . .

. . . on the other hand, the favelas—crowded, nearly ungovernable shantytowns that hundreds of thousands, if not millions, of Brazilians call home.

PERU

Peru, for me, wasn't so much about Machu Picchu and the Amazon—though those are surely among the most incredible experiences to be had on the planet. It's about the faces, the mix of Spanish and Indian . . . the painful history of a continent, cruelty and conquest, lost empires, still visible in a slumped-over peasant, falling out drunk after an afternoon drinking *chicha* . . . the T-shirted adults and naked children of the village of Infierno on the Tambopata River, digging out root vegetables and a few tourist dollars. The rest is flashes: a strange night in the shaman's lodge, middle of the pitch-black jungle . . . stumbling blind through the trees and vines while tripping on *ayahuasca*, the path a river of cutter ants—only to find my then-girlfriend, food-poisoned and apparently near death in a jungle lodge miles from help. The chapped, red-cheeked children in the Andes . . . the stone temples built on improbably high peaks and the unavoidable question: "How did they get that there?" . . . the pleasures of ceviche in a small family-run restaurant in a working-class neighborhood, Sonia, the chef/proprietor, dancing to an out-of-tune piano . . .

Cuzco: In Peruvian tradition, workers could dress up once a year and torment their bosses and landlords in public, taunting them while wearing identity-disguising outfits like these.

The market in Cuzco. In a place where waste is not an option, the local chefs learn to work wonders with the stuff—the hearts, organs, heads, and junk fish—that the first world habitually throws away.

The Tambopata River, outside the aptly named Infierno, a forlorn and impoverished town in the Peruvian countryside. We tend, I think, to romanticize poverty when it's surrounded by natural beauty. Barely scraping by on crops of yucca and corn, this town welcomes the ecotourists who come to gape.

The children of Infierno village bathe and brush their teeth along the banks of the river.

(Above left) On the road to Machu Picchu. At a *chicha* brewery, the crew plays the inexplicable "frog game." There's a series of boxes with different-sized holes, each worth a different number of points. You try to throw a special coin in. You drink lots of *chicha*. Who won? Who knows? (Above right) A family-run fruit and vegetable stand. (Below) Tracey, already altitude-sick and on the verge of vomiting, wanders into a celebration and is dragged into dancing by an enthusiastic local. Apparently, her arm doesn't bend that way.

(Above) Amazonia: Tracey, shooting the "piranha scene," is not amused when I keep throwing meat at her. (Below) The shaman prepares my *ayahuasca*, a powerfully hallucinogenic jungle brew.

Machu Picchu.

FOOD PORN

Los Angeles: In-N-Out Burger.

Japan: Kaiseki meal.

Hong Kong: Roast goose.

China: Noodles.

China: Mise en place.

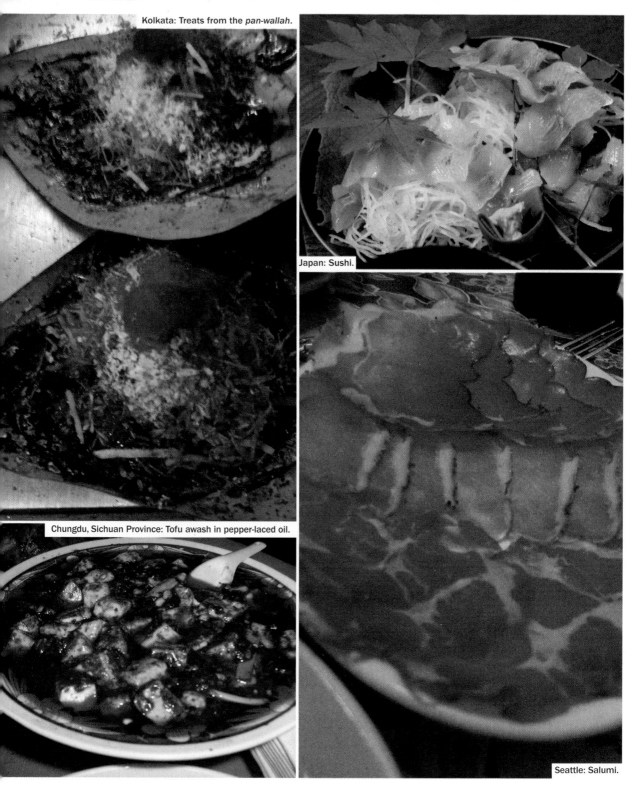

Kolkata: Treats from the *pan-wallah*.

Japan: Sushi.

Chungdu, Sichuan Province: Tofu awash in pepper-laced oil.

Seattle: Salumi.

Korea: Kimchee in progress.

The Sunderbans, India: Prawns.

Rajasthan: *Tali* meal.

Montreal: *Poutine.*

Montreal: Roast maple-glazed pig with gilded snout at Au Pied de Cochon.

Patagonia: Beef.

Singapore: Chili condiment.

Seattle: Salumi.

Korea: "Hangover soup."

Japan: Breakfast at the *ryokan*.

245

Hong Kong: Razor clams.

INDIGENOUS BEVERAGES

It is a pleasant feature of travel that one finds oneself from time to time being offered a local beverage. As guests in rural villages, farming communities, jungle longhouses—places where people work hard and, given the opportunity, play hard—we often become the focus of attention for people who pride themselves on not just their generosity but their traditional booze: usually a home-brewed concoction of near-lethal alcohol content. A bottle, or many bottles, of cloudy rice whiskey, palm wine, grappa, corn beer—anything that can be mashed, fermented, and distilled—is produced, and the locals look on, watching to see if the American TV host and his crew enjoy the proud expression of their cultural heritage. And to see if we're pussies.

It is imperative in such situations to be a good guest. You are not going to make friends in this world if you turn your nose up at the generous offer of a drink. Just because you know that (as in Peru, for instance) the fermentation process began in the mouths of the toothless old women chewing yucca outside the hut where you are sitting, that's no excuse to offend your hosts. And if your intention in traveling is to get on the inside of a culture, you would be foolish to turn down such a gracious invitation of a way in.

In Russia people are not outgoing, or cheerful, or even particularly friendly. The women meet you with a look that says, "I could snap your collarbone without blinking. Why are you here?" And the men are equally gloomy—until you get halfway down the vodka bottle, that is. And you will. There's no way out. Each paint-peeling shot, inevitably from a whole bottle, plunked

down on your table as automatically as the ketchup at a burger stand, is accompanied by a specific toast. To refuse the ninth toast of "To our mothers!" is to say, in effect, "Fuck your mothers." Whatever relationship you might have had with the locals, it ended right there. Stick with it, however, and you are rewarded with a slow reveal of the beautiful Russian soul, a flowering of heartfelt declarations, poetry, song, and expressions of comradely affection. Centuries of Russian history and culture open up to you, make you a part. Soon you begin to understand the magic of the birch forests, the fierce Russian winters, the sad majesty of black crows on snow-covered fields. You vow to reread Tolstoy, to read Gogol—in Russian. Then you throw up in your shoes.

It's like this everywhere. The chief of an Ashanti village is very proud of the jet-fuel-like *apatashi*—a distilled liquor made from palm wine in fifty-five-gallon drums in a jungle clearing behind his court. The man offering you a glass is his minister of war, or his herald, or the keeper of his herds—and you would be well advised to drink deeply and enjoy. You are being watched. Basic decisions about you are being made. To choke, to cough, or, God help you, to decline would be a terrible rejection of the tribe's hospitality and cultural heritage. It is useful to remind yourself in such circumstances that the people offering you a drink have very likely been around longer than you and have a more glorious history, and that you are damned lucky to be where you are and the beneficiary of such kindness.

A teetotaler in Ghana offends not just his host, but the host's father. And his father, and his father's father, going all the way back. A

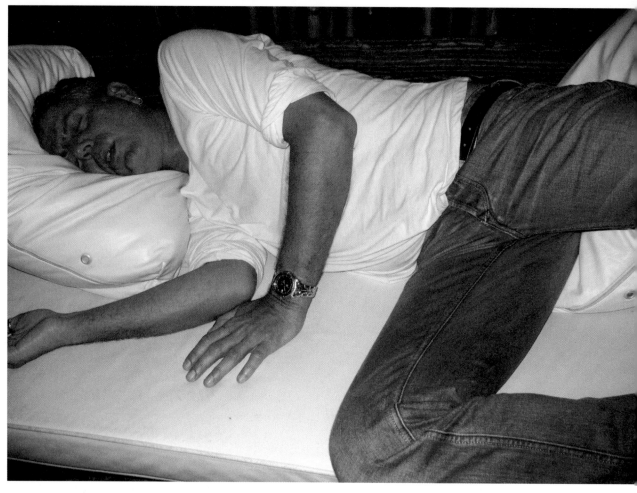

(Above) Brazil: The endless procession of lethal cachaça drinks finally takes its toll. (Below left) Borneo: *Langkau*. (Below right) Peru: *Chicha*.

teetotaler in Japan is a lonely soul, for only through drink will he know the other side of the buttoned-up Japanese. Being drunk in Kyoto is perfectly acceptable—within pre-scribed hours—and, in fact, expected. To *not* get stupidly, embarrassingly drunk in such circumstances just wouldn't be cricket. The Japanese respect team players. And I'm nothing if not a team player.

At a longhouse in Borneo, one of the chiefs reached casually over to me on the matted floor, patted my knee, and said, "You are my brother." This heartfelt, once in a lifetime moment—like so many on the road—would never have happened had I not knocked back many, many shots of my hosts' homemade *langkau*—a particle-filled rice whiskey—killed a pig, and eaten it with them under a single, generator-run bulb. We opened our hearts to each other, as so often happens, over liquor.

Wait, you say. Doesn't fourteen hours of slugging unfiltered Ghanaian moonshine leave you feeling just the teensiest bit under the weather? Well, sure. But crawling home on all fours and waking up feeling as if one's head has been penetrated by angry howler monkeys is a small price to pay for such lusty adventures and touching personal encoun-ters. We—all of us on *No Reservations*—pay that price with pride.

You will notice, in the accompanying photographs, that the members of the crew seem to drink a lot. Understand that in the places we visit, we are all of us honored guests, and as such are received with the finest hospitality that can be mustered. We are very aware of the fact that our hosts are often very poor. That daily life is a struggle. That the food and drink we see before us has been hard won. When an enthusiastic head-hunter, in the middle of filming, offers a drink to a camera person, it is, we have found, more expedient and polite to simply drink it and return to shooting.

Plus, it makes for good TV. One of the things I'm proudest of on the show is how rarely you see our kind hosts freeze up in front of the cameras—intimidated by this strange, invading force. Chances are, that by the time the cameras are rolling, the crew has eaten with their families, played with their chil-dren, hung out in their kitchen, petted their dogs. And had many drinks with them. We are no longer potentially hostile aliens from the other side of the world, bringing the tele-vision lens into their homes and private spaces. We are fellow drunks. Friends, who will show the world how much fun we had in Sichuan Province or the Amazon basin. How proud our hosts were. How generous. How good their food. How they know to party in Sarawak, Borneo!

So, sneer not, dear reader. We are not alco-holics. We are citizens of the world, emis-saries of cross-cultural understanding, ethnologists at work for the good of all men. We are professionals.

Texas: Beer.

Brazil: Caipirinhas.

Texas: Rattlesnake wine.

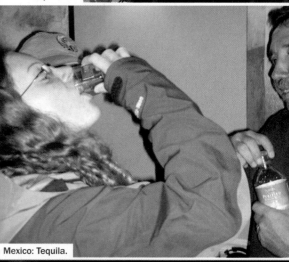

Mexico: Tequila.

China: Shaojiu.

Iceland: Brennivin.

Seattle: Todd Liebler, professional.

Peru: *Chicha* drinker.

Sicily: Grappa.

BATHROOMS
AROUND THE WORLD

When you spend as much time traveling the world as we do, the quality and characteristics of the local plumbing become a constant concern—as well as a major topic of conversation. Without putting too fine a point on it, if a camera person has to break off for ten minutes in the middle of shooting a scene at a roadside restaurant in the mountains of Vietnam, they will, on their return, inevitably be asked: "Well? How was it?" If, as is so often the case, this brief interlude has been preceded by shared distress of any kind, we'll all want to know the particulars. Success? Or failure? A problem? Specifics, please. This is partly the result of a craving for cheap entertainment among five people who spend way too much time together at close quarters. But it is mostly the product of very real concern.

Plainly stated: As we are constantly looking for signs that it might soon be us curled up on a cold tile floor, shaking and sweating and intermittently coughing up bile, we like to stay briefed on the quality of the facilities in which we might be doing those things. There are the basic logistical and practical questions, of course: Should I even bother? Will I need my own toilet paper? Or insect repellent? Would I be better off simply seeking out a bush or a drainage ditch? Or, alternatively, have I found the Promised Land: a clean, well-stocked, reasonably private toilet with good water pressure (not likely to back up and create embarrassing questions about the peculiarities of American digestion)?

These concerns take on an urgency bordering on the pathological when executive producer Chris Collins is along. Among his many eccentricities is a lifelong aversion, surely the result of some early childhood

Malaysia

India

BEST

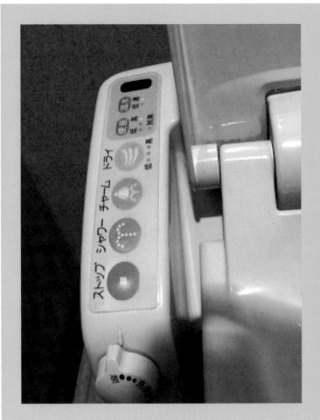

If you're comparing plumbing around the world, there's no contest. Japan wins. The Japanese like to be clean. Very clean. This is a nation of people who advocate showering—and scrubbing with a bristle brush—before getting into the bath. So it's little surprise that their toilets are marvels of technological achievement, announcing the national preference for not only a seat so clean you could eat raw *uni* off it, but a discreet visit—with the sounds of one's efforts masked by cheerful musical accompaniment or a recording of a waterfall. Upon finishing one's business, one may choose from a menu of perineal fountains that direct water of varying pressures and temperatures at one's nether regions. Sit down on a crapper in Japan and you might choose not to get up for a very long time. When you eventually do, the toilet will thoughtfully clean itself.

trauma, to using any toilet within three feet of a bathtub. How to put this delicately? If we find ourselves staying in a hotel where the bathtub is deemed too close, Chris is basically blocked up like the Holland Tunnel at rush hour. Which means we've got to hear about it all day.

Chris's plumbing phobias are complicated by a separate but no less pernicious mania: He is bound and determined to eat spaghetti Bolognese at every hotel in the world—no matter how unpromising and even frightening the prospect. Even in places where they've never even seen an Italian, much less experienced real Italian food, he's got to have it, like some crazed butterfly collector. From

Namibia to rural China, he can't resist the charms of mystery meat *al Italiano*—a compulsion for which he pays a heavy price.

As do we.

Because this is a family book, I'll draw a curtain around the rest of our lavatory exploits (I'm looking at you, Todd "The Pisher" Liebler). But there are nuggets of hard-won road wisdom that we can pass along to you here, the answers to a debate that recurs constantly in the course of our travels: Who has the best—most comfortable, most sanitary, most life-affirming—toilets in the world? And who has the—nightmarish, Boschean, I'll-never-eat-again—worst?

Uzbekistan: Toilet.

WORST

Choosing the worst country for bathrooms is a little harder. While Japanese toilets aspire to a degree of luxury unknown in the barbarian West, the entries at the low end of the scale raise the question of whether they can even be admitted to the category of "bathroom." Is a hole in the ground behind a shed in a Chinese rice paddy a bathroom—or just a place to shit? Is an open space over a river in Borneo a bathroom? Or merely a medieval, gravity-powered privy?

In determining criteria, I arrived at this formula: A "bathroom" shall be described as a space set aside exclusively for the purposes of evacuation and ablution. Within these parameters, then, Uzbekistan wins out over its open-air competition. I would greatly prefer the communal ditch on a pig farm in China, with its advantages of breeze and sunlight, to the less public but infinitely more fetid hellhole that one is likely to find in suburban Samarqand. Remember the film *Trainspotting*? For insight into the wonders of the typical Uzbek bathroom, imagine its infamous "Worst Toilet in Scotland," and know that it looks like a hospital kitchen by comparison. Fighting off carnivorous insects while squatting with one's pants around one's ankles, trying not to slip in the muck while at the same time nervously monitoring the unlocked "door" and tearing a piece out of the local newspaper—this is a skill set one must quickly master in the steppes of central Asia. Most of us just loaded up on Imodium and figured, I'll shit on the plane home. Next week.

COOKS

The old man making stir-fried noodles in a steamy, closet-sized hawker stand on the edge of a housing project in Singapore; the commis, plating and garnishing in the state-of-the-art kitchen of Per Se in New York; the old woman on a farm in the Peruvian Andes, making *cuy*, grabbing a guinea pig from the scores of them scurrying around a straw-strewn room next to her living quarters, skinning it, roasting it over an open fire . . . The pizza maker in Portland, mixing his dough by hand; the old woman in Saigon with a portable kitchen on a yoke over her shoulders: steaming broth on one side, plates and garnishes on the other . . . The newly promoted salad man at my former workplace, Les Halles, a long way from Puebla, where his wife and mother line up with the other women outside a telephone kiosk to call him; the old man in Hong Kong, rocking up and down on a bamboo pole, disfiguring himself for his noodles; the chef in London, tyrannical in the kitchen, shy and ill at ease outside it; the line dogs at the hotels in Milwaukee, Beirut, São Paulo, Melbourne: the same hopeful, haunted look, the same jokes . . . The kid peeling potatoes in the garbage area; the culinary extern getting hazed in his first big-city restaurant; the overenthusiastic young chef, besotted by foam and liquid nitrogen, about to get his first public slap-down in tomorrow's dining section . . . The bakers, the pâtissiers, the

BEING A COOK IS LIKE BEING IN THE MAFIA: ONCE IN, NEVER OUT. WHICH, AS IT TURNS OUT, IS A BEAUTIFUL THING.

garde-mangers, the poissoniers, grill cooks, sauciers, banquet chefs; the invisible ones on the fringes of the restaurant business working for fly-by-night, one-lung caterers, unloading their carefully packed and prepped goods into hot boxes and chafers . . . The short-order cooks, knocking out their millionth order of eggs over easy, toasting yet another English muffin under a salamander, struggling with a waffle iron, scraping Mel-Fry off a filth-encrusted griddle; the "best chef in town" staring at the ceiling in the middle of the night—wondering how to keep it going, to not fall down . . . The rowdy kitchen crew, drinking together at some industry-friendly hangout, residual adrenaline still pumping, the fifth shot of Jäger, or tequila—or Fernet Branca, or Grand Marnier, or whatever it is cooks swill when the shift is over—yet to hit home and send them to bed unsteady, reeling and still stinking of salmon and kitchen grease . . .

So much work. So many random acts of kindness. So many meals—good and bad and indifferent and triumphant. So many smiles, brief expressions of solidarity. And I've been there for so much of it.

A lot of the places we go to make *No Reservations*, they know me. If it's a Western-style restaurant, maybe they've read *Kitchen Confidential*. Other places, they know me from TV—I'm the tall, goofy-looking American guy with the travel show. Invariably, where they don't speak English,

when they want to show me they know who I am, they smile and make an eating motion: "You eat other people's food. Now you will eat mine." Many other times, of course, they have no fucking idea who I am—and could care less. They only know I'm strange—from somewhere else, I'm accompanied by other strangers with small cameras, and that we're interested in their food and what they do—and that my crew seems at ease with the local customs. This is usually enough. There's always a moment—often after an initial hesitation. Maybe it comes once we've eaten the durian—or the warthog, or an offering of a duck tongue, a strip of gut, a bowl of pasta. We get a smile from our hosts, a look of happy surprise. I like to think it says "Oh! You motherfuckers are serious! There's hope for you!" And that's when things shift in wonderful ways—and things get crazy and unforgettable. When they crack open the good stuff, and show us things we might never have seen.

When someone feeds you, they're saying something, they are telling you something about themselves. If you can't hear a voice, or if the voice is confused, chances are, you're eating at a "big box" faux-fusion restaurant—or a chain, or a hotel—where the menu and recipes were arrived at long ago, by consensus or committee. But when you can hear a whisper in your ear with every plate that arrives at your table, or tortilla wrapped personally by your host and placed directly in your hands, a bowl of *pho*,

WHEN SOMEONE FEEDS YOU, THEY'RE SAYING SOMETHING; THEY'RE TELLING YOU SOMETHING ABOUT THEMSELVES.

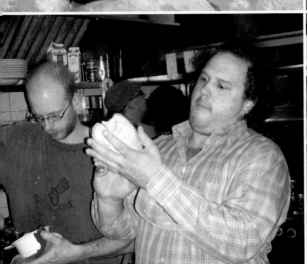

handed to you with a silent grin, then you feel . . . part of something . . . privy to a secret language, an ongoing, worldwide dialogue that's been going on since the very beginning.

From time to time, standing in an airport, some queasy fan will approach me and ask, "How do you eat all that stuff?" I think: So many people are trying to tell me things; why would I want to shut my ears to what they are saying? Particularly these days—when so much of what you hear coming out of people's mouths is bullshit? There is no lying with food. You either can or can't make an omelet. No amount of skill with words can conceal the truth of the matter. If you can cook, your soup is seasoned one of two ways: the way you like it, or the way your guests will like it. Both scenarios contain simple, inescapable truths.

It's funny how it's taken all these travels—so very far from home—to understand how lucky I am to have been a cook, how important that moment was, all those years ago, when I begrudgingly took a dishwasher job in a restaurant kitchen. How different things would have been had I not applied myself to the matter at hand, had I not looked over at the salad man and the fry cook and the broiler position and said secretly to myself, "I want that job." When I dropped out of college and began cooking for a living, it was the first time in my life that I had any real respect for the people around me—or for myself. I worked hard and went home proud. Little did I know where this pirate ship would lead me—or how far.

Being a chef or a cook is like being in the Mafia: once in, never out. And it is a beautiful thing, it turns out, to be a made member of the International Fraternity of People Who Cook. It has enriched my life and connected me with others in once unimaginable ways—as it connects all of us who've ever cooked professionally. Everywhere in the world, wherever people cook, there's a look that chefs and cooks give you that transcends language: It says, "This is what I do. This is who I am. This is where I come from. This is my story—right here—on this plate. Now, try this."

It's good to be a cook.

RESOURCES

WHERE TO EAT

BRAZIL

Bar do Mané
Mercado Municipal Paulistano
Rua da Cantareira 306, Centro
São Paulo
Telephone: +55 11 3228 2141
As "Paulista" as you wanna be. In the Municipal Market, you'll find the hometown favorite, the mortadella sandwich: a steaming heap of thinly sliced mortadella and gooey melted cheese in a soft roll. This and a cold beer are the breakfast of choice for travelers in the know, and an excellent hangover cure as well. The first place I go when in São Paulo—and great street cred when your Paulista friends ask you where you've eaten so far.

D.O.M. Restaurante
Rua Barão de Capanema 549, Jardins
São Paulo
Telephone: +55 11 3088 0761
www.domrestaurante.com.br
Finally, a "best restaurant in town" that actually has something new to say. The shockingly creative menu uses traditional Brazilian ingredients to maximum effect and with maximum skill—like giant Amazonian catfish and varieties of delightful tubers you've never heard of before. If you eat at one fine-dining restaurant in São Paulo, this should be it.

CANADA

Restaurant Au Pied De Cochon
536 rue Duluth est
Montreal, Quebec
Telephone: 514-281-1114
www.restaurantaupieddecochon.ca
Too much is not enough at madman-genius Martin Picard's casual, no-bullshit sugar-shack-meets-French-classic. It's about foie gras here. And pork. And duck and blood sausage and all good things, in get-the-defibrillator abundance. This is a meal you have to train for. And the first place you should go in Montreal.

CHINA

Nanxiang Steamed Bun Restaurant
85 Yuyuan Road, second floor, Huangpu
Shanghai
Telephone: +86 21 6355-4206
Okay . . . it's intimidatingly enormous and crowded beyond belief. The line downstairs for take-out in this unpromisingly touristy area alone might frighten off the less hardy and determined eater. But don't be fooled. This is a respectable choice for best soup dumplings on earth. Order a selection of pork, crab-and-pork, she-crab, and the big bastards—the ones containing only soup. You slurp out the near-boiling liquid with a straw. No matter how carefully you proceed, you likely will burn your throat—but know that any three-star Michelin would be proud to serve a dish this good, this beautifully crafted, and this widely admired.

FRANCE

Chez Robert et Louise
64 rue Vieille-du-Temple
Paris
Telephone: +33 0 1 42 78 55 89
A step into Hemingway's *A Moveable Feast*, a dark, tiny, mostly local bistro with cats and dogs underfoot, where old ladies hack off great hunks of *côte de boeuf*, cook them in an open hearth and serve them on blood-dripping wooden boards. (The *boudin noir* is also excellent.) This is the Paris of dreams, the way you wanted it to be.

Chez Denise (a.k.a. La Tour de Montlhéry)
5 rue Prouvaires, near Les Halles
Paris
Telephone: +33 01 42 36 21 82
Another temple of old-school Parisian bistro classics like *blanquette de veau*, *rognons*, and other enduring glories of French cuisine. Untouched by time, in the best possible way.

GHANA

Asanka Local
P.O. Box LG 634
Legon, Accra
Telephone: +233 021 502715
www.asankaghana.com
Call ahead to get directions, though everyone in the neighborhood will be able to direct you to this classic Ghanaian "chop bar," a popular joint with great live local music, incredible spicy stews and garnishes, and a great scene. Whole families—Mom, Dad, Grandma, and kiddies—dancing and eating and having a good time. A quick, easy total immersion in the best of Ghana.

HONG KONG

Yat Lok Barbeque Restaurant
G/F Po Wah House A, Tai Ming Lane
Tai Po
No telephone
Oh, Lord . . . hast thou created anything better than the truly sublime, multilayered, multidimensional, mind-blowingly good roast pork here? Yes: the roast goose here. So lip-smackingly unctuous, you'll embarrass yourself by moaning obscenely in public.

Tung Po Sea Food Restaurant
Java Road Cooked Food Centre
99 Java Road, North Point (2/F)
Telephone: +2880 9399, +2880 5224
Chef "Robbie" is your guy at the favored choice among many in this wild, crowded, and boisterous *dai pai dong* (cooked-food stall) center. This collection of busy stands, operating on the top floor of a wet market, has

dozens of specialties. Order them all. The fish balls and noodles with squid ink, the "pissing" shrimp, and the pig's feet are mandatory. A good place for a late-night beer-and-food binge, and about as local as it gets. If you miss this on a trip to Hong Kong, you ain't been to Hong Kong.

INDONESIA

Warung Babi Guling
Jalang Tegal San #2
Ubud, Bali, 80571
Telephone: +62 0361 976445
This is it: simply the best goddamn pig in the universe. Whole hog, stuffed with fresh herbs, then lovingly slow-roasted over a low open flame, constantly mopped with coconut milk to crisp its skin. The guts are made into a spicy blood sausage, which alone is reason enough to make the trip to Bali. Kick off your shoes, climb up into the communal dining area, sit down at one of the long, low tables, and dig in. It's a quintessential Ubud experience—and a true "food epiphany." You will never be the same.

JAPAN

Koyoshi
1-3-12 Shibata
(by the Hankyu Umeda train station)
Kita-ku, Osaka
Telephone: +81 06-6372-5747
A tiny, old-school, mom-and-pop, Edo-style sushi bar seating about six or seven. Just sit down and tell them, "You decide," and the proud elderly couple behind the counter will dazzle you with sushi the way it should be made. No frills, no modern takes, just great fish, perfect rice, and lovely, warm people.

LEBANON

Le Chef Restaurant
Gouraud Street
Gemayze, Beirut
Telephone: +961 1 446769
The real Beirut—as it was, should be, and hopefully will be again. A casual local joint/international hangout, notable for its assortment of meze and daily specials. You can't go wrong here.

MALAYSIA

Fish Head Place under the Big Tree
In the front yard of a rundown house across from No. 6 Jalan Tiga (the Khaseng Corporation building)
Sungai Besi, Kuala Lumpur
No telephone
Fantastic steamed fish head and other Malaysian/Chinese specialties, outdoors, next to a noisy metalworking facility. A real "How the hell did you find this place?" local favorite.

Choon Hui Coffee Shop
Ban Hock Road, near Grand Continental Hotel (ask anybody)
Kuching, Sarawak, Borneo
No telephone
I mentioned *laksa* before. Here's my choice for "best": fiery, butt-burning, and made in the city where (arguably) they make it at its highest level. Who knew it could be the breakfast of champions?

PERU

Sonia, Pescados de la Isla
Agustín Lozano La Rosa 173
Chorrillo, Lima
Telephone: +51-1-467-3788
www.restaurantsonia.com
Ceviche, the way it's supposed to be—served by exactly the kind of family-run neighborhood joint you want to enjoy it in.

PUERTO RICO

Lechonera Los Pinos
Carr 184, Km 27.7 Bo Guavate
Cayey, 00736
Telephone: 787-286-1917
Mmmm, pig. Whole, spit-roasted, succulent . . . and the second best I've ever had.

SINGAPORE

Sin Huat Eating House
659-661 Geylang Road, Lorong 35 Junction
Telephone: +65 6744-9755
A crummy-looking yet utterly fabulous "eating house" in the downscale neighborhood of Geylang. One eats seafood here—notably, the sublime crab *bee hoon*, whelks (*gong gong*), prawns, and spotted cod. Warning: A lot more expensive than it looks.

Tian Jin Hai Seafood (ask for Francis Yeo, the Shark Head Guy)
Macpherson Food Center, Stall 13
Jackson Kopitiam, Macpherson Road
Who knew that steamed shark head could be such a revelation? This unassuming stand in the Macpherson Food Center—a colossal megaplex of amazing things you never even considered putting in your mouth—is the place to go. Also the best chili crab I've had in Singapore.

SPAIN

Rafa's
Calle Sant Sebastiá 56 (across from Snack Mar Los Golondrinas)
Roses
Telephone: +34 972 25 40 03
Ferrán Adrià's favorite restaurant: a perfectionist chef-owner, a small counter filled with fish, and a menu of "whatever's good," all absolutely fresh, cooked mostly *à la plancha* and served without adornment. A crankier, more casual, Spanish version of Masa. And if you miss it while in town for El Bulli, you've missed the point.

Pinotxo Bar
Mercat de la Boqueria (near the main entrance)
Barcelona
Telephone: +34 93 3171731
www.boqueria.info

If you know ten people in Barcelona, proprietor Juan should be one of them. Go in the early morning, squeeze onto a stool, and ask what's good. The baby sea cucumbers, cuttlefish, and squid (as tiny as your pinky nail) will change your life. Fill up. Drink. It's only ten A.M. There's plenty of time for a nap.

UNITED STATES

Barney Greengrass, the Sturgeon King
541 Amsterdam Avenue
New York, NY 10024
Telephone: 212-724-4707
www.barneygreengrass.com

Forget what you saw on *Seinfeld*. This is the real New York. Go Sunday morning, wait on line with the *Times* and the *Post* under your arm, and enjoy the eggs scrambled with smoked salmon and onions, the crispy bagels and bialys, and the assorted smoked fish. Be sure to buy some chopped liver to go. It's the best there is.

Yakitori Totto
251 West 55th Street, near Broadway
New York, NY 10019
Telephone: 212-245-4555

I hesitate to mention this place, because until recently, it was a well-kept secret. Other than a few chefs (like Thomas Keller), its clientele was entirely Japanese. Then, Michael Ruhlman foolishly blabbed about the place on his blog. Totto is all about fresh-killed chicken—notably the skin, breastbone, heart, liver, and ass—skewered and grilled to perfection. The Kobe beef tongue is also amazing. It's a step directly into Tokyo, only a few feet off the New York streets. Go early, as they sell out of their specialties quickly.

Masa
Time Warner Center
10 Columbus Circle, fourth floor
New York, NY 10019
Telephone: 212-823-9800
www.masanyc.com

The ultimate in high-end food porn, and probably the most expensive restaurant in America. Sit at the nine-seat sushi bar and let chef Masa Takayama tell you what to eat. While enjoying your meal, know that no one—anywhere on earth—is eating better than you. When I want to reward myself for a nice payday with a totally self-indulgent treat, I take myself to Masa.

Le Bernardin
155 West 51st Street
New York, NY 10019
Telephone: (212) 554-1515
www.le-bernardin.com

As if Eric Ripert and Maguey Le Coze's three-Michelin-star institution needed more praise: For thirty-five years, it's been a veritable primer on how to run a great restaurant. What's remarkable is how relevant it remains. Eat seafood—it's what they do. The meat ghetto on the menu is for knuckleheads.

Katz's Deli
205 East Houston Street
New York, NY 10002
Telephone: 212-254-2246
www.katzdeli.com

When visiting a strange city, eat what they do best. And in New York, we do deli better than anyone. Katz's is the top of the pile when it comes to a heaping, hot, spicy pastrami sandwich.

Sushi Yasuda
204 East 43rd Street
New York, NY 10017
Telephone: 212-972-1001
www.sushiyasuda.com

Best "traditional" sushi in New York. Sit at the bar and order the *omakase*. You'll never be able to eat "utility sushi" again.

Apizza Scholls
4741 SE Hawthorne Boulevard
Portland, Oregon 97215
Telephone: 503-233-1286
www.apizzascholls.com
Get to this place early, 'cause when the hand-mixed pizza dough runs out, they close the doors. (That could be as early as 8:30.) This is purist pizza, made with the kind of obsessive perfectionism that makes Portland one of America's best food destinations.

Salumi
309 Third Avenue South
Seattle, Washington 98104
Telephone: 206-621-8772
www.salumicuredmeats.com
This temple to cured meats is one of my Happy Places, and should be a damned national monument. Armandino Batali and family have done something truly special, and eating here once is not enough. Anything cured or braised—hell, anything they do—is worth trying. A reason for hope in a world of darkness.

Hominy Grill
207 Rutledge Avenue
Charleston, South Carolina 29403
Telephone: 843-937-0930
www.hominygrill.com
Rachael Ray ate here—and it doesn't suck! In fact, it's—dare I say it?—motherfucking yummo. The shrimp and grits here are the best I've had (and I've had a lot), and the "Big Nasty" of fried chicken, biscuit, and gravy is superb.

VIETNAM

Ben Thanh Market
Intersection of Le Loi, Ham Nghi, Tran Hung Dao and Le Lai streets, District 1
Ho Chi Minh City (Saigon)
No telephone
This enticing, chaotic wet market is the first place you should go in Ho Chi Minh City. The food stalls selling local specialties are where the action is. Belly up, point and eat. It's all good! The lady out by the entrance, selling tiny little birds deep-fried in a wok, is not to be missed. *Pho*, spring rolls, hunks of jackfruit . . . it's a wonderland of good stuff and the perfect introduction to a great food city.

Com Nieu Sai Gon
6C Tu Xuong Street, District 3
Ho Chi Minh City (Saigon)
Telephone: +84 8 932 6388
The alternately nurturing and fearsome Madame Ngoc, whom I considered my step-mom, has sadly passed. But her awesome, chaotic restaurant remains. The dining room is a madhouse, an explosion of happily gorging Vietnamese, wildly colorful, flavorful food, and her dangerously airborne trademark: sizzling rice cakes. One of the most memorable meals anywhere.

Anh Tuyet
25 Ma May St.
Hanoi
Telephone: +84 4825 8705
Meals in Madame Tuyet's humble private home in Hanoi's Old Quarter can be arranged in advance. She's famous for her honey-glazed chicken, her house-roasted coffee, and anything else she decides to put on a plate. This is a once-in-a-lifetime dining experience.

HAZARDS

Indonesia has delicious *nasi goreng*. It also has giant, flesh-eating lizards. Malaysia has *laksa*—and leeches. Peru? Amazing ceviche. Also ringworm, typhus, and huge blood-drinking insects that could reduce Ainsley Harriot to a withered husk in a matter of minutes—not that I've thought about it. The world is big and full of wonders, and if you're going to experience them, you've got to be prepared to deal with certain environmental hazards that you wouldn't face at, say, Chili's. (On the other hand, your chance of getting an insipid, soul-sucking, corporatized meal in Inferno, Peru, are close to zero.) So it's the rare episode in which every member of the crew emerges entirely unscathed. Here's a sampling of the risks, hazards, and parasitic nasties that we at *No Reservations* see as a small and fair price for quality travel entertainment.

(Above) New Zealand: I learn how *not* to drive an ATV. (Right) Parasitic or allergic? I have twenty bucks on parasitic. Tracey picked up these strange-looking patterns after shooting in the rain forest in Brazil. She's been too busy or too chickenshit to see a doctor. Diagnosis, anyone? I find the markings too opportunistic and random to be an allergic reaction. Subcutaneous worm?

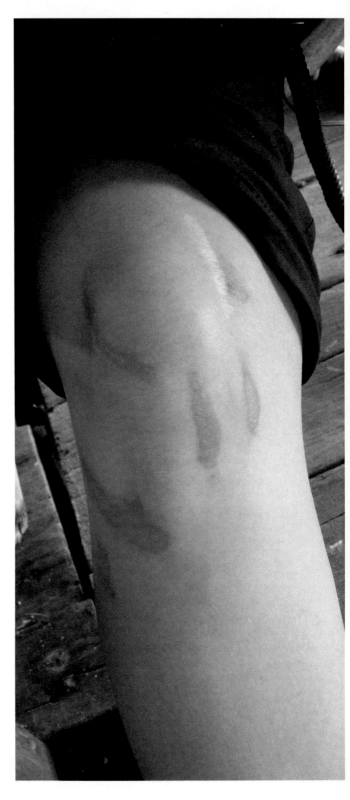

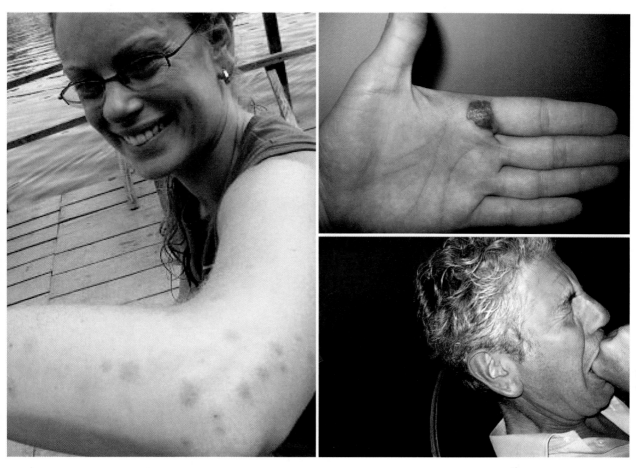

(Above left) Tracey, unusually attractive to any flying, biting insect, shows off the effects of a hard day's work in Amazonia. These nearly invisible little fuckers were all mouth. The bites remained, still itching, a month later. (Top right) India: Diane demonstrates a textbook case of cutaneous larva migrans. (Above right) In India, for unknown reasons, my ear suddenly and painfully swelled to twice its normal size. Ain't travel fun? (Below left) Mexico: Cameraman Jerry Risius has his head wound tended to. When Jerry, shooting at the "Birthplace of the Nacho," walked blindly into a low hanging ceiling, it thankfully interrupted a stultifyingly boring scene-gone-wrong. Naturally, like hungry fish, the other cameras turned immediately on him. We made a scene out of it. (Below right) Namibia: Dr. Liebler conducts field surgery.

TIPS FOR THE TRAVELER

? **RECONNAISSANCE:** Moscow can be a cold, lonely place when you don't know anyone who lives there and speaks the language. So can Tokyo—and Paris, and Saigon, and Borneo. Just about anywhere you go, you're unlikely to experience the "real," everyday flavor of the place if you're just wandering around, reading from the guidebook. So when heading off into this great big world to make another episode of *No Reservations*, we don't go blind—and to whatever extent possible, you shouldn't either.

In making the show, a lot rides on our selection of local "fixer," a person experienced in such matters who can suggest destinations; arrange transportation, clearances, and permits; and generally keep us the hell away from anyplace with a herd of fanny-packers at the bar or a Luau Burger on the menu. We've been fortunate many times in finding good fixers. But we've also had disasters. In one otherwise idyllic Mediterranean country, for instance, every single thing that was supposed to happen went somehow and suspiciously wrong. Our greedy and mendacious fixer would typically take us to the "best" pizza joint in the country—only to have us discover,

between barely edible bites, that he owned the place. Carefully scheduled helicopter rides would evaporate midflight. Giant sea turtles would become too ill to appear on camera. Sea urchin would go suddenly out of season. In these situations, when our fixer falls down, we're on our own. And assuming that you're not lucky enough to have a credulous, deep-pocketed TV company to pay for your guides, you are, too.

But don't despair—and for God's sake, don't give in to the temptation of organized tours. Bus tours, cruise ships, organized, guided forays with set routes and meal times—unless you are physically infirm, they're an atrocity. I like to use the "airplane model" when describing the risks of such enterprises. Imagine you're in tourist class on a plane to Miami. There's the cougher in the seat behind you. The hyperactive, Ritalin- and Game Boy–addled kids across the aisle. The boring blowhard in the next seat who wants to tell you about the miracle ointment that's helping his skin allergies. By the time you hit Miami, you can't wait to get off the plane and away—speeding toward the beach and a strong drink. Now: How would you like to spend the next two weeks living cheek by jowl with this random assemblage of humanity? You wouldn't. But that's what you're signing up for when you take a cruise or a bus tour. And you can't change your mind and get off at will. You're stuck like a trapped rat, moving only as fast as your slowest fellow passenger.

Instead, plan the trip yourself. You can do this. It's not like you're being air-dropped in the bush with nothing but a loincloth and a match. You have any number of invaluable resources at your disposal. Start where the professionals do: with a decent guidebook.

LONELY PLANET: No matter where you go in the world, no matter what remote, ass-backwards, sinister little dunghole you "discover," chances are someone from the Lonely Planet guide has been there before you. Though very useful for fundamentals, the guide is in no way comprehensive (nor does it attempt to be). Hotel suggestions are usually spot on—whether you're talking rural China or urban London. Dining selections, on the other hand, range from excellent and current to sketchy and out-of-date. Not that you should be relying on a guidebook for that kind of thing anyway. Perhaps the best and most enjoyable way to exploit the Lonely Planet guide is by using its restaurant and eatery choices to provoke spirited responses on the Internet. Which brings us to . . .

ONLINE RESOURCES: They're everywhere. In between the credit card scammers and the celebrity crotch shots, the Web is jam-packed with food nerds and food bloggers, food journalists, food obsessives . . . and chefs. Use their strange and terrible powers for Good. Here's how: With Lonely Planet for reference, choose a few typical local specialties for your destination. If planning a trip to Malaysia, for instance, you might select *laksa*, the beloved noodle soup, available in many preferred variations. Now punch the words "laksa" and "best" into your search engine. You will immediately be presented with scores of newspapers, websites, and blogs, each one advocating the "best laksa place ever." Pick one as "yours."

Now visit some foodie websites. Egullet's Asia/Pacific board would be an appropriate first choice here. Oozing certainty, begin a thread titled "Best Laksa in Malaysia!!" describing your "recent experience at the perfect, off-the-beaten-track laksa joint in Kuala Lumpur." Proudly insist that it's The Best—better than any other place you tried. Be sure to misspell a few words—maybe even get an ingredient wrong. Now stand back and watch the fun. Outraged, indignant food bloggers from the U.S., Malaysia, and Singapore who've dedicated their lives to chronicling their adventures in laksa—photographing every order, violently arguing about their choices with other bloggers and journos—will seize on you and your post like enraged seagulls, conveniently disgorging their own experiences at "far superior" and "much more authentic" places in their rush to prove you an ignorant boob. Many will provide colorful descriptions, lavish details of ambience, menus, links to other websites and blogs—and helpful photographs. In an appropriately chastened response, defer to their greater wisdom, and be sure to ask for addresses. If you doubt me, try this with "Singapore" and "chicken rice" then wait for the torrent. (This same strategy is very effective using the words "best" and "dive bar.")

If you're a daredevil, you might reach out directly to the least insane-sounding contacts in the host country or destination and even arrange to meet. But tread carefully here. Being held hostage by some Travis Bickle–esque noodle freak isn't anyone's idea of a pleasant travel experience.

ONCE YOU'RE THERE, THERE'S A HARSH AND SIMPLE RULE TO LIVE—OR AT LEAST EAT—BY: If you see more than two people from your own country or home state in a restaurant, you are in the wrong place. After a half century of experience with itinerant gabachos/gaijin/round-eyes, the proprietors of tourist restaurants have learned to make a deracinated, half-assed version of their own cuisine, because that's what Mr. Ugly Shorts and Sandals likes. Not you. You're an adventurer. Find a place where locals go. Think about it: Of course they know where the good food is. They live there.

If you don't miraculously stagger off the plane and into such a place, visit the central market first. "What do people eat here?" "What do they like?" "What gives them pleasure?" "What's in season?" These are hugely important questions in gaining any kind of understanding of a new culture. And there's no better place to get quick and effective answers than the central market. If nothing else—even if you speak not a word of the language—you'll be able to observe knowledgeable people distinguishing between what's good and what's sublime. Better yet, most of these markets, like Saigon's Ben Thanh, Barcelona's Bouquería, Tokyo's Tsukiji, Singapore's wet markets, and Mexico's mercados, contain or are adjacent to cheap, casual eateries set up for the dining pleasure of market workers. Find one of these places, point, smile, and eat. You can scarcely go wrong. They have regulars to keep happy, and they're close to supply, so the food is almost always fresh and good. Be friendly and grateful, and visibly enjoy what you're eating. You'll be surprised how often a total stranger will approach you to practice English or make suggestions for other places to visit or eat. Listen carefully. And take notes.

Failing this, you can start your research inside the comfy confines of your own hotel. But avoid the concierge like an offer of chlamydia; however well intentioned he may be, he sees it as his responsibility to send you to the "best" restaurant in town. And painful experience has taught him that what the great majority of his guests think is the "best" is a place that doesn't serve anything too "ucky" or "strange." A place that's clean and free of "scary" locals who "talk funny." An "exotic" but comfortingly familiar place where menus are printed in multiple languages and no one ever gets sick. A place with a burger for Junior and a "local specialty" for Dad. Which with grim inevitability means the Hard Rock Cafe or some bogus fusion place where they know they ain't ever seeing their customers again after they drop the check.

You are inquiring of the wrong person.

If you are staying in a large, Western chain hotel (in the completely understandable case that you prefer flush toilets and high-speed Internet), chances are the kitchen staff is headed up by members of the sizable and very savvy subculture of transient chefs and cooks. These guys—mostly Europeans, Americans, and Aussies—move across the globe constantly, transferring from one outpost to another, usually paying close attention to local ingredients (they have to, after all), foodways, and traditions. Chefs know how to eat—and the last thing they want after a hard ten hours on the line is some bullshit version of what they've been cooking all day. Often, at the end of their shift, the kitchen staff—at least the Westerners among them—will gather either at the hotel bar or at a nearby establishment. Find this place. Your concierge, if nothing else, will know where it is. Buy drinks for the chef. And for the cooks. Pump them for information. And when the concierge finally shows up after work, he'll take you more seriously.

If the hotel cooks let you down, there's one more last-ditch option. In just about every city abroad, there's an "authentic" Irish "pub," a "press club," or a sleazy watering hole filled with Westerners and the girls who pretend to love them. In such places they at least speak your language and are often not a little bit homesick and talkative. Though chances are the denizens of this bar don't wander too much from the soccer on TV—and the pints of Guinness and the Bon Jovi on the juke or the Filipino cover band playing Queen songs—they did once. If they live and work in Hong Kong or São Paulo, once upon a time, someone—a local business contact, a girl, a friend—took them out for the real thing. Encourage them to remember, preferably with the aid of several free drinks. Pay particular attention to the guys with local girlfriends.

But no matter how well you plan and research, things will go wrong. The place you end up will not be the way you imagined or hoped it would be. Your local guide will disappoint. The restaurant you heard about will have moved, or changed hands, or burned down. Be prepared to move to Plan B. Even if there is no Plan B. Travel is an amazing privilege and life is short. If you're not enjoying the zoo, abort mission midstream and try something else. Be impulsive. Happy accidents, those perfect meals and experiences, happen only to those bold enough to let them happen. You can't find the perfect meal. It finds you.

Many, many times, while making the show, we have had to divert from a carefully planned itinerary. Being an unusually light and mobile crew, as soon as it becomes apparent that the "smoked fish scene" is neither interesting, nor dynamic, nor authentically regional, we cut our losses and get the hell out of there—as politely as we can and as quickly as good manners allow. To hang on like a dog with a bone, hoping for the best, leads to dispirited, unenthusiastic, and fake television—the kind of painful-to-watch scenes you see on those "Best Of" shows on Food Network, where the food is clearly crap, the place bogus, and the host miserable. We try to make up for our losses by simply keeping our eyes open. Some of the best times, best scenes, and best food stemmed directly from looking out the window and taking an unplanned run at a street vendor, accepting an invitation from a stranger, or just wandering.

So the place is dirty. It's a one-man taco stand outside the market in rural Puebla state. Or a not particularly friendly or hygienic shop with roast geese hanging in the window in Hong Kong. There are dogs, or cats, or chickens running around on the floor, between the legs of the customers. But the place is packed with locals—and they're all eating the same thing. You know what? I'll bet they make a damned good taco. Or goose, or whatever it is they do. The owner of this ancient-looking place hasn't stayed in business all this time by poisoning his regular customers. And tacos, it appears, is what he does—what he's apparently very good at. One chef, one dish. If he's the "goose guy" or the "noodle guy" or the "chicken rice guy," that's his specialty, something he's been doing for years, something he learned from his father or mentor. And the fact that he's busy—in a culture or neighborhood where they know about tacos, or goose, or noodles—says a lot. This is exactly where you should be eating. Find a chair. Order what your neighbor is having. You have arrived.

EQUIPMENT

iPOD: I'm ashamed to admit it, but from time to time, after tens of thousands of miles of traveling, the landscape and scenery, no matter how magnificent, fail to register. Occasionally, even that reach-out-and-touch-the-face-of-God view from eighteen thousand feet up in the Andes becomes wallpaper. Call it fatigue, or being jaded from too much time on the road, or whatever. But the cure is my iPod.

We are all the stars of our own private movie: heroic, tragically misunderstood, and of course, much more sympathetic than we are in real life. And we deserve a soundtrack—loaded with personal favorites from our own emotional history. Stuff that makes us feel weepy or powerful, that reminds us where we came from and how far we've come. When standing on top of Machu Picchu, for instance, jacking a little Depeche Mode into your head adds another layer of poignancy to the experience. Iggy Pop's "The Passenger" makes the long, relatively featureless road from Tashkent to Samarkand much more dramatic. Wagner's "Ride of the Valkyries" is cheesily perfect for a helicopter ride over the Ghanaian jungle. And if you have to endure—as I have—an eight-hour van ride across the Atlas Mountains and the Sahara with a driver whose only tape is *The Best of Judy Collins*, then your iPod is your savior.

BOOKS: Guidebooks, travel essays, and historical accounts germane to the destination at hand are, of course, invaluable. But I also like to bring along those works of fiction that illuminate a locale in ways that nonfiction can't. Doesn't matter if the story is a contemporary one. Does it capture the soul of a place? I read Graham Greene's *The Quiet American* every time I go to Vietnam. Zola's *Belly of Paris* is perfect for that city. Ian Rankin's Inspector Rebus series is marvelous for Edinburgh. And so on. If you're jet-lagged and awake in the middle of the night, a good book is the perfect companion. And it adds something to your trip when you stumble across street names and locations you've just read about.

PLAYING CARDS AND CHIPS: You will most likely be caught in circumstances beyond your control requiring long waits. Your plane will be delayed. Your hotel room will be unavailable. Your bus/car/rickshaw/dogsled/camel train will be late. Nothing like taking your travel companions' money in the meantime.

LAPTOP, HEADPHONES, AND DVDS: Even in the most unlikely places these days, you'll find a wireless signal. In rural China, halfway up the Himalayas, we got better wireless service than in our New York City apartments. More important, you'll need the capacity to play DVDs. It's a long flight to Tokyo or Australia—and how many times can you watch Will Ferrell in an elongated *Saturday Night Live* skit? Be prepared. Bring your own DVDs and the means to play them.

POWER ADAPTORS. Can't charge your phone or your laptop without one. Bring a selection.

ASPIRIN: It's little help for jet lag, but as you will—if you follow my suggestions for intelligent travel—be getting the occasional hangover, you'll need a fistful of these.

IMODIUM (OR LOMOTIL): The traveling foodie's best friend. Diarrhea is the most common ailment of the adventurous eater. Take these as soon as a problem occurs, or even before. If traveling in Uzbekistan, for example, you would be well advised to consider which is worse: to be unable to use the bathroom or to have to use the (fetid pit that passes for a) bathroom. I opt for the former.

TUMS (OR ROLAIDS): Spicy food is good food.

CIPRO (OR SIMILAR ANTIBIOTIC): When all else fails—after a meal of crap-fouled warthog in the Kalahari, for instance—it's time to pull out the heavy guns.

NEOSPORIN (OR SIMILAR ANTIBIOTIC CREAM): Why risk infection if you cut yourself far from any kind of medical facility?

CIGARETTES: Even if you don't smoke, know that a timely offer of a Marlboro (or other widely recognized American brand) can be a potent icebreaker. In many cultures, you will be offered cigarettes. It will be much appreciated if you return the offer with your own. Also invaluable at roadblocks and in encounters with corrupt policemen, private militias, and various and sundry other menacing types. Don't offer them as a bribe, just smile while discussing your situation and casually offer a smoke.

VALIUM (OR SLEEPING PILLS): I have come to see twelve-hour flights as an opportunity to sleep. And I use all the help I can get.

INFLATABLE NECK PILLOW: Particularly on ill-designed American carriers, your head will slide around maddeningly throughout the flight, making it impossible for you to rest. Those silly-looking inflatable doughnuts that wrap around your neck mean you might actually be able to grab a little sleep.

BATHING SUIT: It may be unlikely that you find yourself at the beach when traveling to Russia, but there's the hotel pool—and the very real possibility that you'll be invited to a steam bath or sauna.

COMING HOME

By now, I know every piece of luggage by heart. When our days or weeks in a country are done, we pack our tapes and equipment into two heavy black plastic cases, and our soggy clothes, still reeking of wood smoke and fish, are stuffed into personal bags. Tracey and Todd slide their cameras into carry-ons. Diane strips her hotel room of soap and cosmetics. We load the van and take that last drive to the airport, where we exchange hugs and kisses with our local fixer and our driver and promise to see them again.

There's the by-now-routine passage through security and immigration, and then the five of us find ourselves—yet again—in some characterless airport lounge, drinking beer, catching up on e-mails, making quick phone calls home. We are stuck for an hour or so between the very different parts of our lives. The familiar noiseless, smell-less embrace of airport limbo: not where we were, and yet not quite home.

When you're a tourist on vacation, coming home means coming back to real life: familiar places, relationships, work, love, the rent. The trip becomes capsulized, a series of photographs, a cherished memory—a dream. But when you travel for a living—when "work" is drinking *ayahuasca* with

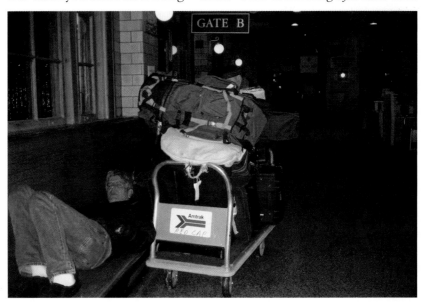

a jungle shaman or standing on a glacier, when you're as likely, on any given day, to be trudging down a riverbed in Borneo as standing on line at Starbucks—you start to ask yourself: Which of these is my "real" life? And if the answer is that the road is the real thing, how do you go back? How do you pick up your old life, your normal life, after you've seen all this?

Returning to grilled cheese and bacon, or even a good piece of fish—sautéed Western-style with a drizzle of butter sauce and a microgreen garnish—seems flat and lifeless after experiencing the colors and condiments of Asia. The expectations of a meal become distorted in fabulous ways after you've learned the sadomasochistic delights—the pleasure/pain ratio—of Sichuan hot pot, the pleasurable scorch of a Kuching-style *laksa*. Salt and pepper just don't do it anymore when you've become accustomed to the wrong-but-somehow-right tang of Vietnamese fish sauce. The squeak of a nicely aged, medium-rare sirloin between your teeth somehow pales next to the sticky lip smack of steamed shark head or pig tail. The clothes you see and wear back home seem shapeless and washed out when you've come to take the graceful silk *ao dai* for granted—or spent too long in a sarong. The clatter of porcelain cups at a Beijing teahouse becomes ambient room noise. The bar at the W Hotel in Westwood starts to seem alien, airless, and sterile. And you fear that one day, you'll look at your old friends and your loved ones and think, "I was sitting under a bouquet of human skulls, drinking rice whiskey and eating wild pig with my new headhunter buddies last week. How do I feign the appropriate level of interest in everyday things?"

It has been said that we find out more about ourselves when we travel than about the places we visit. And it's true that I always look for a universality—some common ground, a unified theory of human behavior. A comfortable takeaway that would describe the world and the behavior of everyone in it.

But maybe you do have to go home, look inward, to find some meaning in what you've seen of the wide world. Staring at my infant daughter while she sleeps, her expression changing second by second as pleasure, fear, concern, and wonder flash across her brain, I find . . . something. I've seen those expressions elsewhere and everywhere. Maybe the differences between places are no less—and no more—pronounced than the distance between human hearts.

ACKNOWLEDGMENTS

Thanks to the people who make *No Reservations*:

Chris Collins, Lydia Tenaglia, Tracey Gudwin, Jerry Risius, Alan Deutsch, Alex Wolff, Todd Liebler, Michael Green, Alan Weeks, Zach Zamboni, Rennik Soholt, Diane Schutz, Tom Vitale, Nari Kye, Chris Martinez, Eric Lasby, Jesse Fisher, Dave Robinson, Robert Quirk, Rob Tate, Mustafa Bhagat, Paul Brandes, Reda Charafeddine, Chris Erdman, Manuel Sander, Toshiharu Takatsuka, Mike Toth, Christina Wood, Jessica Arnold, Eliot Glazer, Adam Lupsha, Kyle Supley, Judah Bauer, Russell Simins, Jon Spencer, Blues Explosion!, Michael Ruffino, the Muscular Christians, Travis Antolik, Steve Beganyi, Chis Mole, Marshall Reese, Matt Foglia, Benny Mouthon, Jared Seidman, Steve Tenaglia, Myleeta Aga, Kya Marrero, and special thanks to Pat Younge, who keeps us safe from Evil.

PHOTO CREDITS

On pages with more than two photos, all credits are listed clockwise from top left unless otherwise indicated.

6: Tracey Gudwin. 8, top to bottom: Diane Schutz, Todd Liebler. 9, top to bottom: DS, TL, DS, Rennik Soholt. 11: DS. 19–24: all photos DS. 25–27: all photos RS. 28–35: all photos DS. 37: TG. 38: all photos DS. 39: DS. 41–49: all photos RS. 50–51: both photos TL. 53: DS. 54: DS, TG, DS, DS. 55, from top: DS, TL. 56–60: all photos RS. 61, from top: RS, TL. 62: RS. 63: TL. 65–67: all photos DS. 68: DS, TL, DS. 69, from top: DS, TL. 70: DS, TG, DS. 71: DS. 72: DS. 75–85: all photos DS. 86–89: all photos Thomas Vitale. 90: TL. 91: TL. 93: TG. 94: both photos RS. 95, left to right: TL, TG. 96: TG. 97: RS. 101–107: all photos RS. 108–112: all photos RS. 116–131: all photos DS. 135: DS. 136–137: TG. 138–141: all photos DS. 142: TG. 144: DS. 145: DS. 146: DS, TL, DS. 147: TL, DS, DS. 149: TG. 150: TG. 152–155: all photos DS. 156–157: Alan Weeks. 158: RS. 159–163: all photos TL. 164–165: all photos DS. 169: TG. 171: Adam Lupsha. 172–175: all photos DS. 176–179: all photos Nari Kye. 180–187: all photos DS. 189–197: all photos DS. 198–205: all photos RS. 206–211: all photos RS. 214–217: all photos RS. 218, from top: TL, RS. 219: both photos RS. 220: TL. 222: TL. 224: RS. 225: RS, TL, RS. 226: RS. 227: RS. 229: TL. 230: RS. 231: RS, TL, TG. 232: RS. 233: TL. 234: RS, TL, RS. 235: all photos RS. 236–237: TG. 238–239: DS. 240: DS, TL, RS, DS, DS. 241: DS, TL, DS, DS. 242: TL. 244: RS, DS, DS, RS, RS. 245: DS, RS, TL, RS, DS. 246: RS. 248–249: all photos RS. 250: RS, RS, DS. 252: RS, RS, RS, DS, RS. 253: DS, DS, RS, AW. 254: both photos DS. 255: both photos DS. 256: RS. 259: RS. 260: all photos DS. 261: DS, RS, DS, RS, TL. 263: RS, RS, RS, DS. 264: RS, TL, DS, DS. 265: RS, DS, DS, RS. 266: DS, RS, DS. 274, left to right: courtesy Discovery, TV. 275: RS, DS, DS, RS, RS. 276: DS. 285: DS.